HR KNOW-HOW IN MERGERS AND ACQUISITIONS

Dr Susan Cartwright is a Senior Lecturer in Organizational Psychology at the Manchester School of Management, UMIST. She is a Chartered Occupational Psychologist and has been conducting research in the area of mergers and acquisitions for over 12 years. She also has extensive consultancy experience in this field and was herself a practising manager for many years. Her scholarship in the field is internationally recognised, and her work has been featured in both *The Financial Times* and *The New York Times*. She is the author of many books, including *Managing Workplace Stress* (1996) with Professor Cary L. Cooper.

Cary L. Cooper is currently BUPA Professor of Organizational Psychology and Health in the Manchester School of Management, and Pro-Vice-Chancellor (External Activities) of UMIST. He is the author of over 80 books (on occupational stress, women at work and industrial and organisational psychology), has written over 300 scholarly articles for academic journals, and is a frequent contributor to national newspapers, TV and radio. His Fellowships include the British Psychological Society, the Royal Society of Arts, the Royal Society of Medicine, the Royal Society of Health, and the (American) Academy of Management. He is President of the British Academy of Management and is a Companion of the (British) Institute of Management. He has been an advisor to the World Health Organization and the ILO.

D1069631

Other titles in the series:

The Institute of Personnel and Development is the leading publisher of books and reports for personnel and training professionals, students, and for all those concerned with the effective management and development of people at work. For details of all our titles, please contact the Publishing Department:
tel. 020-8263 1158
fax 020-8263 3850
e-mail publish@ipd.co.uk
The catalogue of all IPD titles can be viewed on the IPD website:
http://www.ipd.co.uk/publications

HR KNOW-HOW IN MERGERS AND ACQUISITIONS

**Sue Cartwright
and Cary L. Cooper**

INSTITUTE OF PERSONNEL AND DEVELOPMENT

First published in 2000

Design by Paperweight
Typeset by
Action Publishing Technology Ltd, Gloucester
Printed in Great Britain by
the Cromwell Press, Trowbridge

British Library Cataloguing in Publication Data
A catalogue record for this book is available from the
British Library

ISBN 0-85292-634-0

The views expressed in this book are the authors' own and
may not necessarily reflect those of the IPD

**INSTITUTE OF PERSONNEL
AND DEVELOPMENT**

IPD House, Camp Road, London SW19 4UX
Tel: 020-8971 9000   Fax: 020-8263 3333
Registered office as above. Registered Charity No. 1038333
A company limited by guarantee. Registered in England No. 2931892

CONTENTS

ACKNOWLEDGEMENTS

We would like to thank all the organisations with which we have conducted research and consultancy activities over the years and their contribution to knowledge in this field.

Special thanks also go to the individuals (and their organisations) who have contributed to the case-studies presented in this book for their willingness to share experience.

We are also grateful to Margaret Cannon for preparing the typescript and Richard Goff at the IPD for his patience and encouragement.

Sue Cartwright
Cary L. Cooper

1 INTRODUCTION

Mergers and Acquisitions (M&As) have increasingly become an enduring feature of the business world. However, such events still remain a non-routine and challenging occurrence within the lifetime of an individual organisation and its members.

In the last decade, the level of M&A activity has increased substantially, both in size and frequency. Between 1978 and 1988 the value of domestic activity in the UK increased almost twentyfold from £1,140 million in 1978 to £22,123 million in 1988. Although activity levels were dampened somewhat by the gloom of economic recession in the early 1990s, there was a resurgence of confidence in 1995, which has sustained high levels of investment up until the present time (see Table 1).

In 1996, the total value of worldwide cross-border M&As reached a new record of US$263 billion – an increase of 10 per cent on the 1995 figure.

The cross-border M&A market continues to be dominated by the USA, the UK and Germany in terms of the flow of inward and outward investment. Whereas German and French companies were the major buyers of UK firms in 1995, their place was taken by Swiss, Danish and Norwegian buyers in 1996 who collectively acquired nearly US$9 billion of British businesses.

Employee groups which have been the most affected have been those in the service and knowledge-based industries, such as banking, insurance, pharmaceuticals and leisure. Most mega-deals have been in the chemical industry, which in 1996 accounted for a total transaction value of US$19.5 billion. Activity in the insurance sector quadrupled from US$3 billion in 1995 to US$12.8 billion in 1996 and was mainly concentrated in Europe.

Table 1
EXPENDITURES ON MERGERS AND ACQUISITIONS
WITHIN THE UNITED KINGDOM 1980–1997

Year	No. of companies acquired	Total expenditure (£millions)
1980	469	1,745
1981	452	1,444
1982	463	2,206
1983	447	2,343
1984	568	5,474
1985	474	7,090
1986	842	14,935
1987	1,527	15,363
1988	1,499	22,123
1989	1,077	27,250
1990	779	8,268
1991	506	10,434
1992	432	5,850
1993	526	7,063
1994	674	8,268
1995	505	32,600
1996	584	30,742
1997	504	26,382

Source: ONS Financial Stats.

Table 2
CROSS-BORDER DEALS BY NUMBER AND VALUE
($MILLIONS)

Year	Total number	Total Value
1991	4,165	86,209
1992	4,036	127,695
1993	4,249	163,140
1994	5,312	196,334
1994	5,952	229,368
1996	5,500	263,000

Source: KPMG International 1999–05–26

Recent examples include the merger of the Leeds Permanent and the Halifax Building Society to form the UK's third-largest bank and the Royal-Sun Alliance merger which alone affected approximately 24,000 employees. In 1999 the UK pharmaceutical company Zeneca merged with Astra to form AstraZeneca, which at $32 billion represented the third-largest European deal of that year.

M&As are remarkable phenomena not only because of the

high levels of financial investment involved but in terms of their disappointing outcomes. The gains derived from M&A activity are difficult to assess, but research evidence based on a wide range of performance indicators presents a rather gloomy picture in suggesting that, at best, no more than 50 per cent of M&As achieve the level of success initially anticipated (Cartwright and Cooper, 1996; ISR, 1999). Similarly, joint ventures and other forms of strategic alliance record failure and dissolution rates in the region of 40 per cent (*Industry Week* 3 October 1988; Kogut, 1988). Typically, between 50 per cent and 75 per cent of key managers voluntarily leave acquired companies within the first two or three years post-acquisition. It is not uncommon for employee turnover rates to be as high as 60 per cent. Even amongst 'successful' mergers, the stressful nature of the experience has been shown to produce a negative residual effect on the psychological health of employees.

HRM: The forgotten factor in M&As

Although much has been written about the economic, financial and strategic aspects of M&As, it is only relatively recently that research attention has turned to the role and contribution of human factors to M&A performance. Consequently, the crucial role to be played by the HRM function in the effective management of the integration process is often overlooked and undersupported by senior decision-makers. In 'people' terms, M&As are disruptive and can adversely affect the pre-existing employer–employee relationship, both contractually and implicitly. Not surprisingly, M&As have become associated with high levels of employee uncertainty and distress. Ironically, this is occurring at the very time when companies need and expect greater employee loyalty, flexibility, co-operation and increased productivity.

The process of merger is often likened to marriage (Humpal, 1971). On the basis of available research evidence, organisational marriages would appear to fail at not dissimilar rates to civil marriages. In the same way that clashes of personality and misunderstandings lead to difficulties in personal relationships, differences in organisational cultures and mistaken assumptions and perceptions jeopardise co-operation and lead

to conflicts in corporate partnerships. When personal relationships develop problems, it is not uncommon for individuals to
seek expert counselling as a means of resolving perceived
partner incompatibility and disharmony. In describing marital
problems and the role of counselling, Nelson-Jones (1982, 236)
writes:

> Relationships can be complex because of such factors as limita-
> tions of awareness by both parties, overt and covert
> communication, the contexts and rules under which they take
> place and distorted thinking ... [The focus of counselling] is to
> reduce aversive communication, increase helpful communica-
> tion, increase positive behaviours and improve negotiation and
> problem-solving abilities.

Such observations and the need for some objective wisdom or
'counselling' apply equally to most M&A situations. This is a
role which can be valuably filled or facilitated by the HRM
function. The decision to acquire or merge is a singularly
important one, particularly in that it sets in motion a multi-
tude of subsequent decisions regarding staffing issues,
organisational policies and procedures and workplace organisation. Whereas the initial selection decision identifies the
synergistic potential of the combination and the opportunities
for economies of scale, it is the quality and effective implementation of the decisions which follow that determine
whether or not the potential and opportunities are actually
realised. It is important that such decisions are perceived and
implemented in a sensitive, consistent and fair manner; otherwise, there will invariably be internal conflicts and problems
which will distract the organisation from its important external goals. It has been estimated (Davey et al, 1988) that
'employee problems' are responsible for from one third to a
half of all merger failures.

In practice, many HR managers find themselves counselling
the problems of aggrieved or anxious employees on an individual basis in the merger aftermath. However, this tends to be a
reactive rather than a proactive role and rarely encourages the
more anticipatory, directive and strategic role of an 'organisational marriage counsellor'.

This book focuses on the importance and value of developing an informed human resource strategy as a means of overcoming, or at least reducing, the potentially negative impact of such a major change event on employees. Characteristically, the problems of human resource management inherent in M&A situations concern:

❏ dealing with employee uncertainty and stress
❏ maintaining morale and motivation
❏ resistance to change.

We consider the key features to any 'people-focused' strategy are *consultation, communication* and an ongoing mechanism for *monitoring* the integration process and its effects on employees, particularly as it concerns levels of job satisfaction, physical and psychological health and wellbeing.

This book examines what the HR professional needs to know about the people issues during the pre-merger process, during the implementation stage and during the period of consolidation. It is intended to adopt a pragmatic approach to enable HR professionals and managers to assess the importance of the HRM function to the M&A process, and to develop a proactive and comprehensive management strategy with confidence. The material in this book attempts to present examples of best practice in the field. It draws upon recent research evidence and the consultancy activities of the authors combined with the experiences of HR directors and managers who have been directly involved in M&A integration.

References

CARTWRIGHT S. *and* Cooper C. L. (1996) *Mergers, Acquisitions and Strategic Alliances: Integrating people and cultures*. Oxford, Butterworth-Heinemann.

DAVEY J. A., KINICKI A., KILROY J. *and* SCHECK C. (1988) 'After the merger: dealing with people's uncertainty'. *Training and Development Journal*. November, pp57–61.

HUMPAL J. J. (1971) 'Organisational marriage counselling: a first step'. *Journal of Applied Behavioural Science*. 7, pp103–09.

ISR (1996) *International Survey Research Report on Mergers and Acquisitions*. International Survey Research.

KOGUT B. (1988) 'A study of the life cycle of joint ventures'. *Management International Review*. Special Edition. April.

NELSON-JONES R. (1982) *The Theory and Practice of Counselling Psychology*. London, Cassell.

2 DECISION-MAKING AND NEGOTIATION

The early stages

Many behavioural scientists have argued that the success rate of M&As would greatly improve if more account was taken of the degree of cultural or organisational fit which exists between the buying and selling firms or merger partners. Evidence from studies such as that conducted by John Hunt at London Business School (Hunt, 1988) support the notion that more successful acquisitions are made by acquirers who are well informed about the organisation and have effectively 'stalked their prey' over a relatively long period of time. Prior experience of working together through joint venture and other forms of collaborative agreement has forged links which have led to a number of successful, more permanent organisational couplings, eg Fujitsu-ICL. The exit costs of terminating a 'trial marriage' like a joint venture are considerably less emotionally and financially damaging than a divestiture or the break-up of a merged company.

The decision-making process

In reality, in almost all transactions the decision to buy is based on two criteria: projected earnings potential and strategic fit. Factors relating to human issues are invariably regarded as post-acquisition details for operational management to sort out.

Typically the decision-making process proceeds through four stages:

❏ a decision to acquire or merge is made at board level

- identification/screening of potential targets
- the Due Diligence process
- bidding and negotiation.

A decision to acquire or merge is made at board level

The rationale for the decision will be based on economic and financial grounds, eg to increase shareholder wealth, as a means to access new markets or to acquire new products, technologies or expertise.

This may mask the 'true' unstated psychological motives for the decision, which may be initiated to satisfy the personal whims or egotistical needs of a singularly powerful individual or a collective influence.

At this stage, knowledge of the decision to acquire or merge will be cloaked in secrecy and will not extend beyond the decision-making circle at the very top of the organisation – who may be making decisions about operations and business units outside their own country.

Identification/screening of potential targets

A search for potential acquisition targets or merger partners is then initiated. Often the chairman or CEO will already have a preferred target in mind. Typically, financial and market analysts are briefed to put together a potential 'hit list', utilising computer-based research. Some unofficial approaches or 'sounding outs' may be made very discreetly and a shortlist drawn up. Usually this consists of not more than five candidates.

If the acquisition target or potential merger partner is performing well financially, it will serve to reinforce decision-makers' assumptions that because there are no problems in terms of 'human issues' now, there will be none in the future.

The Due Diligence process

The objective of the Due Diligence process is to investigate the target in more detail, with particular emphasis on its legal and financial health, and its strategic match in terms of products, markets, geographical location, etc. This information will be weighed against factors such as availability and price. The Due Diligence procedure is conducted by a team of accountants and lawyers who report to the board.

At this stage the process is still regarded as highly confidential, although one or two key individuals within the organisation may form part of the Due Diligence team – eg senior personnel in finance or operations management and the managing director designate of the new company.

Certain impressions about the culture of the acquisition target are likely to emerge during the Due Diligence process but are unlikely to influence the buying decision, even if they were to ring some warning bells. By this stage, the decision-makers will have already invested a significant amount of time and money, and will be unwilling to say no and pull out of a potential deal now. They may have become aware of the existence of other potential buyers in the market, which will enhance the attractiveness and desirability of the target – perhaps even to the state of obsession.

During the Due Diligence process, visits may be undertaken to the premises of the acquisition target. This is the stage at which rumours are likely to circulate and may be the point at which vague feelings of distrust and anxiety start to develop amongst employees. This may lead to closer scrutiny of managerial decisions, behaviours and habits by employees in the target company. Normally 'open' managers may be seen to be becoming more closed and guarded in providing information. Decisions to 'freeze' recruitment, run down stocks and suspend training programmes will be interpreted as signs that changes are on the horizon.

Bidding and negotiation

This final stage of the process is concerned with closure and is typically characterised by a competition in negotiation skills between buyer and seller. It is the time when the fun really begins and the parties bargain to broker some form of pre-nuptial agreement. Both parties engage in ritualised game playing in which winning is all important – winning on price, winning on contract details, etc. And even if you are on the 'losing' side, you may have the opportunity to gain personally by 'winning' an attractive exit package or golden parachute. Clashes of personality are likely to override any potential clashes of organisational cultures.

Because the negotiation phrase is almost exclusively about bargaining, the rationale and logic of the decision to buy is never likely to be called into question.

The negotiation period is often both stimulating and exhausting. According to Searby (1969), because so much energy is expended in closing the deal, the acquiring management are often left too exhausted and apathetic to manage the integration process effectively.

Without doubt, the reluctance of decision-makers to withdraw from negotiation has lead to many poor and unsuitable organisational marriages, particularly where talent is the major asset that is being acquired. However, as the case-study below illustrates, some organisations are brave enough to do so and recognise the longer-term advantages and wisdom of that decision.

Case-study

UNCOMFORTABLE BEDFELLOWS

The merger between the Leeds Permanent and The National and Provincial Building Societies

The Leeds Permanent Building Society was formed in 1848. In common with other societies, the prospect of growth by M&A had been discussed and debated at various times throughout its history. Indeed, there had been brief talks with the Bradford-based National and Provincial back in the 1970s.

In 1993, Mike Blackburn, the chief executive of the Leeds Permanent, left to join the Halifax Building Society and an external search began for his replacement. David O'Brien, the contemporary chief executive of The National and Provincial was identified as a leading candidate, the idea of a merger between the two societies took hold, and merger talks got under way. In August 1993 it was announced that the Leeds and The National and Provincial were to merge. At the time, with a workforce approaching 7,000 employees the Leeds was approximately twice the size of The National and Provincial.

In the period of in-depth talks which followed the announcement, it became clear that as well as differences in size there were also significant differences between the two cultures. When Mike

Blackburn had joined the Leeds as CEO six years earlier, he reportedly described it (Pugh, 1998) as 'warm and comfy – nice people, but a bit lacking in cutting edge'. Blackburn was enormously successful in re-energising the Leeds culture to make it more responsive and customer-oriented.

The culture of The National and Provincial was radically different. Whereas the Leeds achieved its success through conventional techniques and 'straight talking', the strategies and ways of doing business that The National and Provincial adopted were generally regarded as unorthodox in comparison with other organisations' in this business sector. Despite its Yorkshire roots, the culture and language of The National and Provincial was more 'Boston' than 'Bradford'. It was characterised by a strong desire to satisfy and please the customer above all else. Trained counsellors were employed in the mortgage arrears department to ensure that borrowers were treated with empathy. The culture and language of The National and Provincial drew heavily on sporting analogies, employees were referred to as 'players', supervisors were renamed 'coaches', and discussion and debate were initiated by 'players' making 'challenges'. To be part of The National and Provincial and its culture, organisational entrants had to effectively learn a new language. Rather than going to meetings, employees attended 'understanding events' and assumed job titles such as 'manager for customer engagement'.

As merger discussions continued, it was clear that managers within the Leeds Permanent were becoming increasingly uncomfortable and frustrated with the culture of The National and Provincial. Furthermore, it was becoming difficult to agree upon a mutually acceptable business plan which bridged the two cultures. After several months of negotiation, a decision was made to abandon the proposed merger. Both Leeds Permanent and National and Provincial subsequently went on to find new partners.

Source: Roger Boyes, chief financial officer of the Halifax Building Society, previously CEO of the Leeds Permanent.

The Role of HRM

Getting involved early

It is still rare for HRM professionals to be actively involved in the decision-making and negotiation process, but it is important that they assert the expertise and value they can add by becoming involved at this early and critical stage. HRM has a number of key roles to play, which involve *counselling, advising, facilitating* and *information-gathering and planning.* The role of HRM can be summarised as being:

- to assess the suitability of the match in terms of factors which extend beyond those covered by the Due Diligence procedure and to be prepared to act as 'cautionary counsel'
- to raise awareness of the people issues and collect as much information as possible relating to human resources
- to identify potential problems and areas of difference between the two organisations which may be barriers to integration
- to begin the process of bringing the new management teams together and clarifying their intentions post-acquisition/ merger.

Cultural fit

The concept of organisational culture has continued to attract the attention of practitioners and researchers of organisational behaviour more generally for some time. The concept has been variously defined (Martin, 1985; Schein, 1985). However, central to most definitions is the notion that culture concerns symbols, values, beliefs and assumptions which operate often in an unconscious way to guide and influence behaviour and to maintain regularity and order. In simple terms, culture equates to 'the way things get done' in an organisation and is the social glue that binds organisational members together. Importantly, because culture operates in a taken-for-granted fashion its value and importance to individuals is often only recognised when it is threatened in some way.

The culture of an organisation is communicated in a variety of observational ways such as its physical layout, structure and style of work organisation, rituals and organisational folklore. It is also reflected attitudinally in the way in which the organisation responds to its internal and external environment in key areas of organisational activity, like risk-taking, decision-making, control and autonomy, tolerance of ambiguity and customer service.

Morgan (1986) focuses on the 'metaphor of culture' as a

shared sense of reality. Those who do not possess compatible cultures do not share the same sense of reality as such, and cannot therefore enact reality with each other. For this reason M&As represent a major organisational event to employees: they threaten and disturb organisational cultures, lead to misunderstandings and often force the integration of people who do not share the same reality.

The closeness of the culture fit is important to M&As because effective integration will invariably depend upon:

either
the extent to which the acquirer or dominant merger partner is successful in imposing its culture on the acquired company or other merger partner
or
the extent to which the two cultures fuse and blend together smoothly.

If the desired outcome is cultural absorption or assimilation, then a good culture match is likely to occur when the culture of the acquirer or dominant partner presents a more attractive alternative to that which currently exists, or is at least acceptably similar. If the desired outcome is cultural integration, a good culture fit can be said to exist when the combining cultures share a significant number of key values, and any cultural distance between the two can be bridged by negotiation or collaborative problem-solving.

One of the key roles for HRM is to make an initial assessment of the degree of culture fit which exists between the two organisations, given the desired mode of acculturation. This may mean being prepared to challenge the suitability of the marriage by quietly, but assertively, assuming the role of devil's advocate. The role entails asking questions which refocus decision-makers on the initial reasons and objectives behind the decision to buy, and at the same time reminding them that there are other alternatives (eg new start-up opportunities in greenfield sites, joint ventures, other targets). Such an approach can be particularly useful at crucial times in the negotiations when obsession and the 'must have' mentality obscures all other considerations.

Sources of cultural data

While it may not be possible to conduct any widescale and systematic pre-acquisition 'culture audit' or appraisal in these early stages, some initial overall impressions of the culture can be gleaned from observations and background research.

According to Edgar Schein (1985), organisational culture is reflected in a number of directly observable ways. For example, the physical environment, the feel and layout of an organisation can communicate a lot about its culture. Taking afternoon tea at a high-class London hotel or department store is a rather different experience from dropping by for a snack at your local fast-food outlet, which illustrates the contrasting cultures, values and priorities of two different types of organisations operating in the retail food and drink sector.

Taking tea at the Ritz is an unhurried affair, ceremoniously and sedately delivered by black-suited waiters against a backdrop of comfortable, traditional furnishings and quality tableware. There is an ambience of almost respectful silence punctuated only by the murmuring of discreet conversations between fellow patrons. The experience is designed to make the customer feel privileged and special, and reinforces the values of hierarchy and status.

In contrast, customer service at McDonald's is geared to delivering a fast, competitively-priced product of a consistent quality to all its customers in a standardised way. Customers collect their purchases in cheap disposable containers from a counter staffed by predominantly young, uniformed 'crew' members. These purchases are consumed in relatively noisy, clean, functional surroundings which discourage 'loiterers'. The experience emphasises the informality, fast pace and egalitarianism of modern-day life and its associated values.

Similarly, grandiose offices and reception areas which display mementoes and pictures commemorating past achievements and former leaders reflect a culture which values tradition, formality and respect for authority. Modern, bright and minimalist environments often intentionally suggest an efficient, informal and forward-looking organisation. Organisations which maintain 'executive-only' dining rooms and other restrictive facilities and privileges reflect a strong need to promote status and high power distance, whereas an

open-plan office arrangement which places a manager along-
side his or her team members is indicative of low power
distance and a more informal open culture.

Other observable ways in which culture manifests itself
include:

- the way in which people interact, their forms of address and
  the language they use

- dress code

- the way in which work is organised and conducted, eg
  production-line assembly versus cellular team arrangements

- the organisation's self-image and the dominant values it
  espouses, often through its mission statements, company
  and product literature

- the way in which it treats its employees and responds to its
  customers – again this is often reflected in the physical
  facilities provided by the organisation

- the rules for playing the organisational game, eg the types of
  behaviours associated with being a 'good' employee or effective manager.

Although it may not be possible for a representative from HRM
to personally conduct an observational analysis of a potential
acquisition or merger partner, this information can be gathered
by:

- questioning members of the negotiating team with direct
  experience

- making subtle enquiries of shared customers/suppliers

- talking to employees within your own organisation who
  may have had contact or experience with the target organisations, eg people who may have previously worked or
  considered working for the target organisation

- using your own professional HRM networks.

Literature sources

Much can be learnt about organisational culture by researching the organisation's history, background and corporate philosophy in order to reach an understanding of its values and priorities. Public information, product literature, corporate mission statements and recruitment material are often useful sources for this purpose. Admittedly mission statements have increasingly become rather bland and tend to reiterate somewhat predictable espoused values which differentiate little between organisations. However, some mission statements clearly communicate a culture such as that of the Co-operative Bank which is strongly driven by its ethical stance and is consistent with the founding principles of the Co-operative movement established by the social reformer Robert Owen.

Employee newsletters, briefings and company magazines are also a valuable data source. The way in which an organisation communicates to its members reflects not only its priorities and values but also its willingness to openly share information, its underlying assumptions about employees and the importance it attaches to communication. This is conveyed in a variety of ways by the informational content, the type of language used, communication style and presentational qualities. Professionally produced employee publications suggest that the organisation takes employee communication seriously. Organisations with task-driven or team cultures tend to communicate using an energising language and tone. Knowledge of the existing communication processes of the acquired target is invaluable in planning a merger-related communication strategy and is discussed in detail in the next chapter.

Personnel data

The most salient issues raised by employees post-acquisition/merger relate to the impact of the ownership change on existing terms and conditions. Again, the HRM function should gather as much relevant information about employment policies and practices as possible ahead of time. It may be helpful to draw up a 'wish list' of information that would be useful to HRM and present this to the negotiating team. The 'wish list' might include:

- basic demographic information such as gender, age profile, tenure, location, qualifications
- staff turnover and absenteeism rates: high turnover and absenteeism rates may be indicative of cultural dissatisfaction and people management problems
- details of existing training courses
- employee handbooks, manuals and HRM policies particularly as concerns pension scheme arrangements and reward systems
- current mood/rumours circulating.

Identifying potential problems and areas of difference

Initial, essentially impressionistic analysis of the culture and HRM practices of the acquisition target may immediately highlight a number of potential problems and areas of difference. These need to be raised with the senior management team prior to the acquisition or merger and discussed in the context of their future intentions and integration objectives.

It is also important to check out these assumptions in more detail once the acquisition or merger has been finalised, particularly as concerns the existence of subcultures, which may be strong in different parts of the organisation. A number of areas in which organisations differ in their attitudes and behaviours have been consistently identified by researchers (Davis, 1968; Harrison, 1972; Deal and Kennedy, 1982; Hofstede, 1990). These cultural typologies will be discussed in more detail in Chapter 7. However, as a starting-point, the main areas can be summarised as being:

- *attitudes towards risk-taking and tolerance of uncertainty and ambiguity*

  Organisations with a low propensity to take risk tend to strive to maintain the status quo and are resistant to change. Organisations with a low tolerance for uncertainty and ambiguity tend to be slow to make decisions and often overemphasise the importance of detail and implementation at the expense of a more strategic focus and approach.

❏ *time horizons*

This dimension relates to the time an organisation is content to wait to realise a gain on its investment. Time horizons tend to be determined by factors such as ownership, type of industry and national culture. Private sector organisations in the UK tend to be dominated by managerial thinking which is distinctly 'short-termism'. This contrasts with Japanese-owned organisations which tend to take a much longer-term view on investment returns. The speed of product development and the acceptable time to market varies considerably between industry sectors. Computer software manufacturers are dependent upon getting products to markets very quickly out of fear of obsolescence. In contrast, for health and safety reasons, product development in the pharmaceutical industry is highly regulated and is a significantly slower process.

❏ *power and control mechanisms*

This refers to the extent to which authority, information and responsibility is delegated and shared within the organisation. Organisational charts, job descriptions and documentation relating to appraisal systems can provide some insight in this area. Command and control management systems are likely to have formalised channels of communication and clearly defined job descriptions and responsibilities.

❏ *levels of employee participation and consultation*

Organisations which limit power and influence to a few key decision-makers tend to be faster and more flexible in their decision-making process than organisations with a more consensual style. Differences in levels of employee involvement tend to also be reflected in communication structures and processes. Past employee attitude surveys can be useful sources of data for the acquiring HRM function in providing some indication of employee levels of satisfaction with organisational processes and work conditions.

❏ *business drivers*

The business drivers can also be a fruitful area for comparing companies. Organisations differ in terms of the emphasis placed on different organisational functions. This is often reflected in formal and informal reward systems. An organisation which conducts regular surveys of customer satisfaction levels, yet neglects to make similar enquiries amongst its own employees and/or invests minimally in the area of employee welfare, clearly reflects its emphasis on the external environment.

❏ *problem-solving strategies*
Organisational cultures evolve through adaptation to the internal and external environment and are the outcome of learning. Areas of difference can often be revealed by the way an organisation approaches a problem. In the context of personnel selection, the value of situational interviews as a means of assessing the 'person–organisation' fit has been increasingly recognised. A similar technique can be employed in the context of M&As to uncover the way in which an organisation has learnt to behave when confronted with a problem. This type of information can be elicited by the negotiation team through the presentation of critical incidents or 'what if' scenarios.

Differences in all of these primary cultural dimensions are potential barriers to integration. However, in the context of domestic mergers and acquisitions research suggests (Cartwright and Cooper, 1996) that resultant cultural changes which are perceived as increasing employee autonomy and participation meet with less resistance than changes which are perceived as increasing individual constraints.

Forward planning

The HRM function has an important facilitatory role in bringing together the new management team and initiating forward planning. As the negotiation period draws to a close, provisional plans need to be made regarding:

❏ selection procedures and employment contracts

❏ the formation of a steering committee/merger management team to assume overall responsibility for the integration process

❏ the handling of the announcement and what will happen on 'Day 1'

❑ the need to involve external consultants to provide specific expertise in areas such as merger re-selection decisions, communication, etc

❑ the location of the new 'corporate' headquarters and organisational name

❑ the organisation of team-building events and specific training initiatives, eg culture workshops and seminars.

As a first step the HR manager needs to initiate a planning meeting with the acquiring/merger management team to discuss these issues. It is also important to clarify amongst team members their plans and intentions for the new organisation and to agree a coherent strategy. Otherwise, not all the members may be pulling in the same direction and this will create organisational confusion. Such meetings need to be carefully facilitated. Any dissent amongst team members has to be confronted and resolved. Otherwise, silent dissent will lead to false consensus and will be manifested in conflicting behaviour.

At the same time, attempts should be made to explore with the team members their perceptions of their own organisational culture as well as that of the proposed acquisition or other merger partner. It has been consistently demonstrated that many cultural change efforts stumble from the outset because management have not established their cultural starting-points. In other words, they have not sufficiently considered what they are in relation to what they want to be. Experience of working with senior management teams suggests that it can be useful to explore culture perceptions using projective techniques, ie by asking members to describe the two combining cultures in terms of an animal or car and to explain the reasons for their choice. In the case of a merger some years ago in the brewing industry (Cartwright, 1998), the senior management team accepted that the cultural size differences between the two organisations were so great that it was tantamount to merging a bear with a fish. The larger merger partner, 'the bear', was slow to respond to its environment but had been protected by its size and presence in the market. It also offered a paternalistic protection to its employees. Employees were well cared for in terms of benefits and opportunities for self-development and the organisation had a people-oriented management style. In contrast, the smaller partner, 'the fish', was a lean, flexible organisation geared to efficiency. However, its attitude towards its employees and the management style it encouraged was rather cold and impersonal.

The 'car' metaphor can also be used to good effect. Information regarding the priorities and functional emphasis within an organisational culture can be extracted by asking probing questions about the specific features of the car – eg who/what would be the driver, the engine, etc? Is the technical specification more important than the comfort features or the way the car looks, etc?

The importance and scale of pre-planning activities are illustrated by the case-study below and provide a useful model.

Case-study

THE ACQUISITION OF BOOTS PHARMA

In April 1995, Knoll Pharma – part of the large German organisation BASF – acquired Boots Pharma, a part of the UK Boots Group. Knoll Pharma had a global workforce of 7,500 prior to the merger. The acquisition of Boots increased this figure to 12,000. Over the five-month negotiation period, Dr Katharina Beyling-Vaubel – an HR manager – played a major role in pre-planning the merger integration strategy.

From the outset, a Merger Steering Committee comprising senior organisational members was appointed and assumed overall responsibility for the merger process worldwide. The Committee was headed by Dr Thorlef Sprickschen, the CEO. There were nine organisational team members, representing global functions, which included R&D, marketing and sales, communication and human resources, plus an external consultant. The Committee met regularly to supervise and monitor progress against merger synergies. The Steering Committee appointed a two-tiered structure of merger management teams. A series of functional global teams were set up to co-ordinate and integrate the merger at a transnational level. Cross-functional regional teams were also formed in Europe and the USA to integrate the merger at a more local operational level.

In addition, Knoll decided to assign 'ambassadors' to each of the operating countries for a period of six weeks following the formal announcement. The role of the ambassador was to provide on-site

Figure 1

THE POST-MERGER-PROJECT-ORGANISATION CREATED TEAMS TO ACCOUNT FOR THE INTER-NATIONAL AND CROSS-FUNCTIONAL NATURE OF THE MERGER

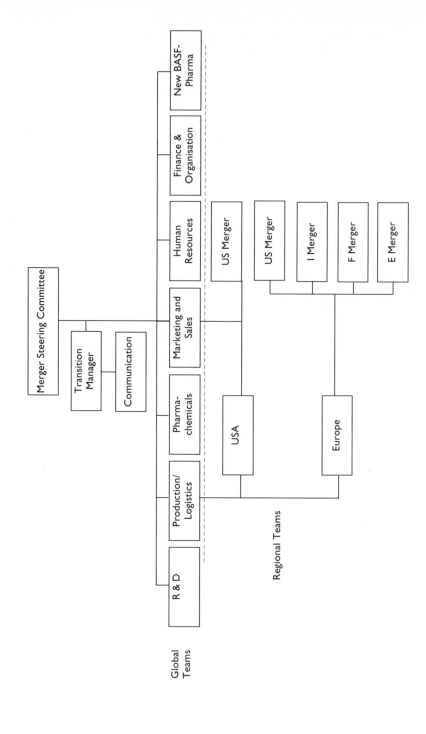

support, to mediate the local decision-making process, to channel communication and to ensure that budgetary and financial controls were maintained locally. The role was akin to being a 'gatekeeper' in that the ambassador acted as a key liaison-point between Germany and the acquired sites. The role was primarily created so that Boots employees would not feel overwhelmed by visiting personnel or be inundated with requests for information from Germany. Decisions regarding the selection of these ambassadors were made during the pre-planning period and were based on linguistic competence and experience of working in other cultures.

Plans were also made regarding the reselection process of the general managers who were to lead the organisation in the various operating countries. External academic expertise was recruited to design fair and appropriate assessment procedures.

The planning process involved the design and organisation of a series of cross-cultural seminars and workshops for senior managers to increase their understanding of their own cultural paradigm and to raise their awareness of areas of potential cultural difference. These were facilitated by external experts. Thought was also given to creating opportunities for joint conferences and meetings between representatives of the two organisations in the early days post-acquisition.

Implementing mergers is about getting people to work together effectively. Anticipating problems and areas of difference and potential conflict from the outset is key to the integration task. Good communication lies at the very heart of the process and is discussed in the next chapter.

References

CARTWRIGHT S. (1998) 'Mergers and acquisitions: the case for an organisational marriage counsellor'. *Journal of Professional HRM*. 13. pp10–16.

CARTWRIGHT S. *and* COOPER C. L. (1996) *Mergers, Acquisitions and Strategic Alliances: Integrating people and cultures*. Oxford, Butterworth-Heinemann.

DAVIES R. B. (1968) 'Compatibility in corporate marriages'. *Harvard Business Review*. 46. pp86–93.

DEAL T. *and* KENNEDY A. (1982) *Corporate Culture: The rites and rituals of corporate life*. London, Penguin Business.

HARRISON R. (1972) 'How to describe your organisation's character'. *Harvard Business Review*. May/June. 5(1). pp119–28.

HOFSTEDE G. (1980) *Culture Consequences*. London, Sage Publications.

HUNT J. (1988) 'Managing the successful acquisition: a people question'. *London Business School Journal*. Summer. pp2–15.

MARTIN J. (1985) 'Culture collisions in mergers and acquisitions', in P. J. Frost, L. F. Moore *and* M. R. Louis (eds), *Organisational Culture*, London, Sage Publications.

MORGAN G. (1986) *Images of Organisation*. London, Sage Publications.

PUGH P. (1998) *The Strength to Change*. London, Penguin.

SCHEIN E. H. (1985) *Organisational Culture and Leadership*. San Francisco, CA, Jossey-Bass.

SEARBY F. (1969) 'Control of post-merger change'. *Harvard Business Review*. September–October.

3   COMMUNICATION

Mergers and acquisitions are emotive events which affect everybody and create an expectation of change. Both researchers and practitioners in the field of integration management emphasise that the ultimate success of a merger or acquisition is determined by the way in which the transition is managed in the first three months (Barrett, 1973; Kingsley Lord, 1996). In the case of mergers it is often difficult to physically integrate the two companies within such a short time-frame. However, it is important that the proposed future changes are outlined as early as possible.

It is also recognised (Kanter, Stein and Jick, 1992) that communication is the key tool within any change process. Colin Ions, executive director for human resources at the time of the Courage-GrandMet merger, was responsible for the company's communications strategy and advises that in M&A situations, 'you cannot over-communicate'. If communications are irregular or poorly co-ordinated, people imagine the worst and the rumour-mill becomes the best source of information.

The handling of the acquisition or merger announcement is the first important task faced by those responsible for making the acquisition or merger a success. The announcement and the way it is handled is critical because it is the primary source of 'official' information that the acquired or merged workforce will have about their future and about the culture of the organisation they will be expected to integrate with or adopt. At the same time, internal communications need to be co-ordinated and consistent with external communications to press, customers and suppliers.

Planning for day 1

An 'acquisition announcement' symbolises the end of a company as its members knew it. It is a time for reflection and assessment. From the acquirer's point of view, the announcement is a celebratory event, marking the completion of a long period of negotiation and anxiety. It is important to remember that in mergers as well as acquisitions there is always perceived to be a 'buyer' and a 'bought'. Whereas acquirers are keen to look to the future and bury the past, those who are acquired prefer to look back to the predictability and comfort of former times. Typically, what the new management wants to communicate is that 'from now on things are going to be different'. In contrast, acquired/merged employees want reassurances that they are valued, their skills are not redundant and that they will still have a job. The handling of the merger/acquisition announcement requires sensitivity to achieve an acceptable balance between what management want to say and what employees want to hear. Typically, what goes wrong is that initial communications create disbelief and anger, or set up expectations which cannot be fulfilled.

Many large organisations employ external consultants to help plan and co-ordinate their communications strategy. This is often desirable, particularly if it is an international merger and/or requires a technological method of delivery. The use of external consultants has the advantage in any change initiative of introducing a balanced and objective perspective which draws on the experience of other organisations in similar situations. To their disadvantage, external consultants may lack sufficient specific knowledge of the organisation and its culture to be able to present a course of action which is accepted as being credible by a critical mass of people in the organisation. External consultants are frequently accused of seeking to drive through initiatives which are politically naïve and then withdrawing from the organisation. If an organisation decides to employ external consultants to handle merger-related issues, it should ensure that they work collaboratively with organisational representatives and that responsibility is shared. It is important to avoid the common pitfalls that management often make in abdicating organisational responsibility and assigning contentious or potentially unpleasant tasks to external consultants.

In terms of pre-planning, the merger planning team needs to consider various questions:

- ❑ Who will communicate? Do they have the required skills? Are they empathetic communicators?
- ❑ What will they communicate?
- ❑ How and where will they communicate? What facilities will be required? How will the process be co-ordinated to ensure that employees are informed at the same time or in advance of any press release?

The case-study below illustrates the importance placed on communication in the AstraZeneca merger, and particularly the use made of new communications technologies.

Case-study

COMMUNICATIONS – ONE OF THE KEYS TO MERGER SUCCESS: ASTRAZENECA

In the merger of two pharmaceutical giants, Astra AB of Sweden and Zeneca Group Plc of the UK, it was decided at the outset of discussions to ensure that the communication system between the two organisations was fully open. Indeed, a major communications exercise, including a dedicated Intranet site, was launched to keep all employees up to date with developments as they occurred in the proposed merger. Recognising that the announcement of the proposal would result in uncertainty about the future in the minds of many people, efforts were made to avoid morale-sapping speculation by making as much factual information as possible available to staff. In a letter to announce the 'merger communications centre' website, the new AstraZeneca chief executive Dr Tom McKillop wrote: 'We strongly believe that during the process leading up to the merger and integration of AstraZeneca that the new website will be important. It is our intention to provide regular material for it.' 'Communications' included the facility for recipients to place a 'merger news' icon on the PC start-up screens, giving them easy access to the site. In addition to being an information source, the site provided a facility for dealing with any questions that employees had.

From the early days of merger discussions up to and after the merger itself, communication has been a high priority with AstraZeneca. Indeed, the new chairman of the company, Percy Barnevik, in a major address at a business school, outlined that one of his major objectives is to 'communicate often and with clarity and passion'. He also added that 'to manage, you need open and honest information'. This has been the hallmark of the newly founded company, so that the merger communications centre has continued as the AstraZeneca communications centre through the Intranet. This information gateway provides extensive information about all parts of the new business, from information and activities of the integration office to the international policies of the company. Organisation charts have been posted, and questions have been put by employees and answered by appropriate senior executives. Such honest and interactive communication helps to prevent the spreading of rumours and myths, to reduce employees' fears and to prevent potentially negative consequences' arising. It also helps to surface specific issues and concerns that trouble people, and allows senior management to deal directly with them.

Of course, not all staff have direct and easy access to the Intranet. In addition to the Intranet site, a corporate integration newsletter, *AZ Update*, was created. The main purpose of this publication is to explain the way in which the company is expecting to operate. It sets out, amongst its objectives, the informing of staff about the progress of integration and responding to the main questions people are asking. It also highlights and explains new business developments, displays the combined company's portfolio of products and helps staff feel that their communications needs are being met. The *AZ Update* has been made available in English, in Swedish and on the Intranet. The editorial team have also worked with *AZ News* (the US newsletter), also published on a fortnightly basis, to provide materials regarding US operations. Besides regular interviews and features, in each issue a feedback section enables employees to identify which articles they found useful and also to identify topics they would like to know more about in the future.

In the first article in this communication, Gunner Christiani, the executive vice president with responsibility for AstraZeneca human resources, shared his vision of 'a company in which our ability to innovate and grow and continue to be successful is directly linked to how people feel about the organisation'. He underlined the importance of communication as a means of dispelling rumours and helping people to understand what will happen next. 'Our best hope of getting this right is to explain, explain and explain again what we are doing and why.'

Although AstraZeneca is essentially a merger of two companies, one Swedish and the other British-based, Swedish and British staff make up only about a third of the total staff. As a result, communication pathways have had to extend around the globe.

AstraZeneca has striven to speedily be one company, recognising that not everything will be perfect first time round. An important message from the chief executive Tom McKillop running throughout all the communications is the formula that the new organisation should be 'fast, fair, flexible and forgiving'.

Source: Dr Eric Teasdale, director of corporate health and safety, and Dr Richard Heron, principal medical officer, AstraZeneca.

Based on the experience of AstraZeneca and other organisations in similar circumstances, the main elements of any communication are likely to include:

❑ a General Announcement statement delivered by the CEO and/or representatives of senior management
❑ more specific local presentations by departmental/line managers
❑ newsletters and other types of merger-related publications via a wide range of communications media
❑ the creation of centralised mechanisms for dealing with employee concerns and problems.

General announcement

Potentially shocking information is better communicated face-to-face than by letter or general notices to staff. It is usual for the CEO of the new company to make a general announcement. To ensure that everybody is informed at more or less the same time, many large organisations find it most practical to produce an employee video which can be shown in the presence of local management. Time needs to be allocated to this task well in advance to brief all those involved. The CEO's statement can be quite brief – about 10 or 15 minutes' duration. However, employees should be given the opportunity to ask questions. Because employees may be reluctant to speak out directly at such events, it may be useful to provide them with a pencil and paper so that they can prepare and submit any questions or issues they might wish to raise anonymously.

The tone of the announcement should communicate an optimistic but realistic view of the future, without appearing overcritical or dismissive of past endeavours. Following an acquisition or merger, a new 'psychological contract' between the individual and the new company has to be established. The announcement should lay the foundations for the renegotiation of that contract by *reducing uncertainty*, increasing employee perceptions of the *honesty and trustworthiness* of the company and reassuring employees that the company has *clear leadership and direction*. Research conducted in the USA (Schweiger and DeNisi, 1991) has demonstrated that employees who received realistic and extensive communication about the merger were less uncertain and had greater trust in the organisation than colleagues who received minimal information. Moreover, job satisfaction also returned to pre-acquisition levels much quicker amongst those who received extensive information.

In terms of the content and structure of the initial announcement, it is therefore suggested that it might include:

❏ a clear statement of the rationale and objectives of the merger or acquisition and the perceived advantages to both parties at an organisational and personal level. People buy into change when they can see personal benefits in doing so – eg enhanced career prospects, increased job security, opportunities for greater involvement, skill enhancement or job variety.

❏ an acknowledgement of the strengths/past achievements of the acquired company. If one organisation has acquired another, it must recognise some existing or potential value within it – even if it was underperforming: eg a good customer base, a technology or product it has or is developing, a loyal workforce, etc.

❏ clarification of the terms of the marriage contract and an explanation as to the direction of future change. The terms of the relationship must be defined from the outset. Is it a traditional marriage in which one partner will assume dominance over the other? Is it a modern or collaborative marriage in which the partners will work together to complement each other's strengths and weaknesses? Or is it an open marriage in which differences in corporate personalities and cultures matter little and will be retained just as long as the acquired company achieves the required targets? A message that presents an acquisition situation disguised as a merger may portray a misleading impression of the power and cultural dynamics of the combination, which may prove an obstacle to integration.

❑ information about what will happen next
❑ a commitment to communicate regularly on merger/acquisition-related issues
❑ an acknowledgement of the importance and value of people to future success, and an appeal for patience in the inevitable confusion and teething problems that will follow.

Specific local information/presentations

In addition to the generic information, employees will expect more detailed information as it concerns their specific site or department. This is best delivered by local management in the form of a series of small group presentations. The purpose of these presentations should be to highlight how the merger or acquisition will affect people, both now and in the coming months, and to outline the timetable for change.

It is important that the information given at any employee briefing is accurate and consistent, to avoid distortion. Managers who are responsible for employee briefings should be provided with clear guidelines and documentation, perhaps in the form of a prepared set of overheads or slides. There are three main areas to be addressed:

❑ jobs and locations
❑ terms and conditions
❑ pension arrangements.

A well-organised presentation will firstly outline those areas in which there will be no change; secondly, those areas in which some change has to be made; and finally, those areas in which policies are still being developed.

From experience, one of the most important issues is pensions, for new employment contracts will involve decisions regarding the transfer to a new scheme. Any information provided at the initial employee briefing will have to be supplemented with more comprehensive information and independent pension advice. When BASF-Knoll acquired Boots Pharmaceuticals (see Chapter 2), in the month following the announcement they ran a series of pension briefings and independent pension advice clinics provided by external experts and produced a number of information leaflets.

Newsletter and merger-related publications

The language of merger-related communications should be unambiguous and explicit. Oral communication will need to be reinforced with written documentation, which employees can consult to ensure that their understanding is correct.

As discussed, organisations must communicate regularly even if the content of the message is only to reaffirm that at the current time there is little or no information to communicate. Communication voids have a tendency to be filled by negative rumours. The usual way to provide employees with regular updates on merger progress is by dedicated merger newsletters. For example, Courage-GrandMet produced its *Integration News* update every two weeks in the early months and also launched a new monthly company magazine. This magazine was significantly different in format and layout from its former publication to emphasise to both employee groups that this was a 'new' company for all concerned. Again, it is important not to focus exclusively on internal matters but to also report external activities and achievements, to reassure employees that the organisation has not become so preoccupied with the merger that it has 'taken its eye off the ball'. As well as the more traditional methods of communication, organisations such as Glaxo Wellcome made extensive use of electronic media, eg videotext/worldwide web and satellite broadcasts to inform their global workforce.

In common with other organisations, Glaxo Wellcome also

produced an integration manual for managers, which as well as providing information on HRM policies and practices included sections giving advice to managers on delivering bad news and managing stress.

Mechanisms for dealing with employee concerns and problems

The questions which employees raise vary little across M&A situations, and in the main are easy to anticipate. It is useful, therefore, to prepare a catalogue of standard answers which managers can familiarise themselves with before they deliver their presentations. The most frequently asked questions are listed below:

The merger

Who will be responsible for the merger process?
How will the new company look?
Will there be site closures?
When will the company stationery and business cards change?

Employment conditions

How will my terms and conditions change?
When will I get a new contract?
What if I am made redundant?
Will existing bonuses/share option schemes be maintained?
Will sick pay arrangements change?
Will we still have the same employee/welfare facilities?

Performance appraisal

Will current appraisal systems remain?
Who will appraise me?
What will happen to performance-related pay?

Redundancies

Who will be made redundant?
Which kinds of jobs are likely to go?
What kind of severance package will be available?

Relocation

Will I be forced to relocate or be made redundant?

Training and development

What will happen to existing training provisions?

Recruitment

Will there be a freeze on recruitment?
What are the equal opportunities policies?

In addition, some organisations set up telephone hotline services to respond to any merger-related issues which management, employees and customers might wish to raise.

There are other forms of help and support that an organisation can provide for its employees at this time – eg stress counselling services – and these are discussed in more detail in Chapter 5.

References

BARRETT P. F. (1973) *The Human Implications of Mergers and Takeovers*. London, Institute of Personnel Management.

KANTER R. MOSS, STEIN B. *and* JICK T. (1992) *The Challenge of Organisational Change*. New York, Free Press.

LORD K. (1996), presentation by Neil McEwen of Director Kingsley Lord's 'Integrating functions between culturally different organisations', ICM Mergers and Acquisitions: The Human Impact Conference, Selfridges Hotel, London, January.

SCHWEIGER D. M. *and* DENISI A. S. (1991) 'Communication with employees following a merger: a longitudinal field experiment'. *Academy of Management Journal*. 34. pp10–35.

4 HANDLING JOB INSECURITY, PAY AND BENEFITS

Many modern mergers and acquisitions are defensive in nature, and are a response to factors such as contracting markets, excess capacity and rising research and development costs, rather than being a strategy for business extension. Consequently, M&As invariably lead to job losses and redeployment as a result of rationalisation and role duplication. In the USA alone, more than 5 million white-collar jobs were lost during the 1980s as a result of corporate restructuring or 'downsizing' (Cascio, 1993).

Usually, financial analysts will have already set targets for 'head-count reduction' at the pre-acquisition/merger stage. However, it is unlikely that firm decisions will have been made as to the exact areas and specific job-holders that will be affected. It is common practice for the responsibility for realising these reductions to be devolved at a local level, and for the area management team to draw up an integration plan which will deliver the required savings. In some cases, financial incentives (ie personal bonuses) may be offered to senior managers to achieve these cost reductions within an agreed time-frame. As is therefore not surprising, M&As make everybody uneasy about their job security and adversely affect morale and motivation levels. This is often described as the 'fear-the-worst syndrome'. Researchers have consistently concluded (Cartwright and Cooper, 1996; Schweiger *et al*, 1987; Altendorf, 1986) that a great deal of merger stress is created by uncertainty and fear of the unknown rather than by change itself. The period following a merger announcement or rumour is one of personal risk analysis and self-appraisal. It is a time when individuals feel extremely vulnerable. In a relatively short time, the stress of uncertainty can often erode any initial positivity there may have been towards the merger, as people feel obliged to passively wait and see what is going to happen to them. In an effort to regain personal control of their circumstances, some individuals may seek alternative employment and physically remove themselves from a stressful situation.

Poor morale and worry may have a pronounced effect on productivity at a time when the organisation is particularly vulnerable to attack from competitors. An employee involved in the Getty-Texaco take-over in the 1980s (Altendorf, 1986) described the demotivating effect of the event on himself and his colleagues in the following way:

> People didn't work – they just sat around. It's one of those things that snowballs. When everybody is down and out and depressed, others get depressed. I don't think any work got done. Employees who would never consider 'stealing' from the company began to take plants, stationery, pictures and books.

In the early days post-acquisition/merger, personal survival becomes an obsession and employee anxieties centre around the issues of 'Will I have a job?' 'Will I have to relocate?' 'Is my current lifestyle in jeopardy?' Because the psychological contract which determines the expectations between employer and employee is broken, the relationship regresses to an essentially financial arrangement or transaction. In motivational terms (Maslow, 1971; Herzberg, 1966), the basic lower-order, physiological and safety needs of employees are activated and predominate over any higher-order growth needs such as challenge and autonomy. Until these 'hygiene needs' have been satisfactorily resolved, motivation and satisfaction levels are unlikely to increase. The challenge for the HR manager is to take steps to alleviate some of the anxiety associated with uncertain job future and ensure that the re-selection and redundancy procedures are handled in a fair and sensitive way. At the same time, senior management need to maintain high visibility rather than retreating to closed meeting-rooms where they may be thought to be secretly hatching unpleasant merger plots.

Organisation structure

It will take sometime to flesh out the details of the new organisation structure, a process that is likely to require the formation of task-force teams to review the activities and practices of each business area. Members of the task-force teams should be drawn from both parties and report to a central co-ordinating committee or senior merger management team. From the outset, the merger management team should set and prioritise the integration tasks it seeks to achieve, and identify the areas in which changes or head-count savings are required. For most organisations, corporate services and sales are obvious targets for rationalisation. Because this will be equally obvious to those who work in these functions, there is little point in attempting secrecy.

Consultative reviews of areas in which job losses are likely should assume priority and be undertaken as quickly as possible. Individuals are more likely to accept hard decisions if they feel that they have been consulted and participated in the decision-making process. Similarly, employees who work in areas of the business which will be unaffected by job cuts should also be informed of this as soon as possible and so be liberated from any unnecessary anxiety. Any review of operations necessitating decisions which involve the closure of one site in preference to others, or the continuation of one research project at the expense of several, may benefit from some external assessment or criteria. This will not only reduce the likelihood of territorial battles but will provide a rational justification for the decision made which can be communicated to employees.

Job losses

Head-count savings can be achieved by means of natural wastage, voluntary early retirement schemes and a freeze on recruitment, or by encouraging employees to transfer to another site or department. In addition, it may be worthwhile offering employees the opportunity to job-share or work part-time, so that they can perhaps return to educational study or undertake some form of retraining, the costs of which the organisation might consider meeting in full or in part. However, all these methods may prove insufficient and a redundancy programme may have to be introduced.

Redundancy is an unpleasant and potentially expensive business. Nevertheless, if critical decisions have to be made regarding head-count reduction, it is usually less painful for all concerned if such decisions do not drag on too long. Similarly, it is preferable for an organisation to make a single cut than to find itself in a position of having to announce several rounds of redundancy over a relatively short period of time. Once redundancies are announced and remaining employees recognise that they have survived, their confidence about their job future returns and they may start to become more optimistic. A subsequent lay-off announcement will destroy that still fragile confidence and any developing trust in the new company. Redundancies which are handled badly may damage corporate reputation and attract adverse publicity. Survivors may also experience feelings of guilt. The emotional and psychological impact of redundancy on those who are released and those who remain should not be underestimated, and will be discussed later.

Severance packages

It is the responsibility of the HR function to negotiate the details of the severance package in compliance with employment legislation and any local arrangements. In addition, the HR function has to consider other ways in which it can offer assistance to those who are to leave the organisation.

The Redundancy Payments Act 1965, which was incorporated into the Employment Protection (Consolidation) Act 1978, sets out the minimum statutory payments. However most organisations offer employees more generous severance terms than those provided for by the Act. Because payments vary from sector to sector, it may be worthwhile taking advice as to the typical level of severance payments offered by other organisations. Incomes Data Services may be a useful source to consult. Employment law various considerably from country to country. It is unfortunate that in international mergers and acquisitions, factors relating to employment law can significantly influence closure decisions. For example, it is apparently easier and less costly to make employees redundant in the UK than it is in Germany.

Communicating redundancy

Redundancy announcements should be planned as carefully as M&A announcements (see Chapter 3). It is better if the person making the announcement is somebody known to the workforce rather than someone unknown sent from Head Office. If the numbers involved are relatively small, it may be possible to conduct individual 'release interviews' rather than make a general group announcement.

In terms of content and structure, general announcements of redundancy should include:

❑ a statement giving the rationale and business reasons for having to take this action

❑ an explanation of why there is no alternative and of the ways in which management have explored other options

❑ an acknowledgement of the service that employees have provided to the company, and that most importantly it is the job, not the individual, that has become redundant

❑ some information on what happens next.

According to Max Eggert (1991), although decision-makers tend to prefer to announce redundancies on a Friday, it is preferable to deliver bad news on a Tuesday or Wednesday. This has the advantage of giving HRM professionals the opportunity to respond quickly and effectively to the many issues that arise immediately afterwards. It also spares employees from a weekend of anxiety and worry about issues which they can do nothing about until the following Monday.

The role of the departmental/line manager

As with M&A announcements, it is important to allow employees who are being made redundant the opportunity to ask questions. Any general announcement should be followed up with a small group discussion or individual interview with the department/line manager, to provide those who are leaving with more specific information. Again, many of the questions which will be raised can be anticipated in advance and the managers involved appropriately briefed. This will increase manager confidence and ensure that all employees receive consistent and accurate information.

Common questions include:

- What will I get paid?
- Can I appeal against the decision?
- How will this affect my mortgage?
- What will happen about my company car, health insurance, etc?
- Why me? How was I selected?
- When do I have to go? Can I say goodbye to my colleagues?
- How will I get another job?
- What will I say to my family?

In recognition that this is an unpleasant and stressful task for managers, it may be worthwhile providing some training and support to help managers to fulfil this role.

Forms of assistance for employees

Employees who leave the organisation can be offered assistance in a variety of areas including:

- personal and career counselling
- job search and assistance
- retirement counselling
- financial planning.

If significant numbers of people are leaving the organisation, it may be worth considering developing a specific programme which could be delivered in-house or be provided by external outplacement consultants, of which there are currently more than 120 in the UK.

The type and scope of services provided by outplacement consultants vary considerably from one-to-one executive counselling to running job-shop facilities and interview training and advice sessions for large groups of employees at all levels. Therefore the selection, design and delivery of an appropriate outplacement programme will take some time and careful thought. When interviewing potential outplacement consultants, Max Eggert (1991) suggests as a starting-point that it is important to consider:

❑ previous industry experience

❑ the kind of resources that are on offer

❑ the exact nature of the services that can be provided

❑ evidence of previous success – ie the percentage of the released workforce in similar assignments who have secured new jobs in the first three months

❑ the pricing structure.

Personal and career counselling

Job loss can present an opportunity for re-appraisal and a chance to make a fresh and invigorating start. However, it is unlikely that the majority of those who have been made redundant will see it that way, even if they have lost a job that they did not find particularly enjoyable.

Individuals who have been made redundant may find it easier to cope if they understand the emotional cycle associated with the event. Similarly, if their managers are also made aware of this cycle, they are likely to benefit from this knowledge.

Employee response to job loss is not dissimilar to other loss events such as bereavement, and is conceptualised as a four-stage cycle of shock, anger, depression, and adjustment.

Shock

The initial surprise or shock of losing a job typically causes an individual to 'freeze up' and be unable to make plans. A common response is to minimise or trivialise the event. Many may even procrastinate about seeking advice or help. Some individuals may have difficulty telling their family and friends.

Although it is necessary to give individuals time to recover from the initial shock, some intervening help may be needed to move individuals on from this stage. Periodically the HR manager or line manager should actively review with individuals the plans that they are making for the time when they leave the organisation.

Anger

After initial shock come anger and bitterness. Typically this will be directed against the organisation, but often spills over into family life. The individual's behaviour is often irrational and may be characterised by sudden and frequent outbursts of temper. Hostility may be targeted against the line manager or the HRM department for choosing the individual in preference to others. Hostility and accusations may also be directed at 'surviving' colleagues, which may arouse feelings of guilt.

Depression

After anger come depression and withdrawal. Sometimes depression may be preceded by what is termed the 'fantasy effect' or 'avoidance behaviour' whereby the individual refuses to accept the reality of what has occurred and becomes preoccupied with rescue scenarios which are unlikely to happen – eg winning the lottery or getting one's old job back. Depression is a normal sequential part of the adjustment process and needs to be recognised as such. However, individuals who experience severe depression are likely to need professional help and referral to counselling services. Again in this respect it can be useful if managers are briefed to recognise the symptoms of depression and are fully informed about the potential sources of help which can be made available. This is a role which can be taken up by occupational health or the HRM function.

Adjustment

With time and the understanding and the support of others, the majority of individuals will adjust to their new circumstances. In this respect, hearing about the positive experiences of those who have faced similar circumstances and have successfully coped and moved on can be very encouraging. The HR manager may be able to identify some such role model and perhaps invite them to speak to employees when the timing is appropriate.

Embarrassment and feelings of guilt can be powerful inhibitors on behaviour. It is not unusual to find that friendship patterns and informal work-group behaviours change when redundancies have been announced. For example, traditional seating arrangements in the works canteen may change: the survivors may choose to eat their lunch with other survivors rather than with members of their work group who are leaving. It is difficult to maintain an inclusive work culture at this time, but efforts should still be made to continue to involve everybody in the social aspects of work. If an individual who is leaving has been an active member of the company's sports team or theatre club, he or she should be encouraged to continue that membership after leaving if he or she so wishes. Sadly, during the redundancy period, many individuals experience intense feelings of physical and psychological separation from the organisation which emanate from the behaviours of those around them. When the actual departure date arrives, it may go unmarked by any organisational ritual or farewell event. Departing employees may believe that others are relieved to see them go. Many organisations worry that if they stage a farewell party, departing employees will behave badly, drink too much and/or act aggressively. In most cases these fears are unfounded.

Many people would welcome the opportunity to say goodbye at a social gathering as opposed to quietly and apologetically slipping away. Rather than assuming how employees want to leave the organisation, HRM should consult with those involved and try to accommodate their wishes. Well-planned farewell parties communicate to those who remain that the organisation is genuinely sorry to have to let people go and that it appreciates their past endeavours.

Tea and sympathy alone is insufficient to help most individuals to cope with redundancy. People also need practical help to increase their self-esteem and find alternative employment. For individuals who have lost jobs in a declining or rapidly contracting industry, it stands to reason that they are likely to experience difficulty in finding alternative jobs in that same industry. Career counselling can provide the stimulation and help which individuals need to realistically identify alternative job and career options. In working with individuals to identify their personal strengths and achievements, counselling can positively enhance self-concept and help employees to regain a sense of control over their lives.

Assistance in this area can be offered as part of a redundancy programme in a number of ways, by:

❏ providing access to one-to-one career counselling based on an assessment process which involves in-depth interviews and the completion of psychometric tests and questionnaires

❏ providing employees with careers literature and information: it might be useful to link up with local employment and training agencies or to invite a representative from the Training and Enterprise Council or the small business adviser from the local bank to speak to employees

❏ running individual or group sessions on self-development, perhaps built around self-help manuals like *Build Your Own Rainbow* (Hopson and Scally, 1993) or *What Color Is Your Parachute?* (Bolles, 1995).

Job search and assistance

Organisations can provide practical assistance to help employees to network, make job applications, prepare their curriculum vitae and improve their interview techniques. Again, this could be provided in the form of a training programme or information leaflets. Outplacement agencies will set up job-shop facilities on the organisation's premises which provide the staff and resources to help the job search process. Such facilities could also be run in-house.

Retirement counselling

Not everybody leaving the organisation will necessarily be looking to re-enter the world of work. It has become increasingly recognised that even giving up a job voluntarily requires systematic preparation and professional advice if individuals are to cope effectively with their change in lifestyle. Retirement also impacts upon other family members, and so many retirement counselling programmes involve the individual and his or her partner.

Financial counselling

Both retirement and redundancy arouse financial concerns and require advice from experts on investments and long-term planning. When an individual becomes unemployed there is no way of knowing how long it will be before he or she finds another job. This presents major dilemmas concerning decisions to cut back on expenses, sell assets, renegotiate loan arrangements, etc, at a time when people feel emotionally vulnerable.

References

ATTENDORF D. M. (1986) 'When cultures clash: a case study of the Texaco takeover of Getty Oil and the impact of acculturation on the acquired firm'. August dissertation. Graduate University of Southern California.

BOLLES R. N. (1995) *What Color Is Your Parachute?* Berkeley, CA, Ten Speed Press.

CARTWRIGHT S. *and* COOPER C. L. (1996) *Mergers, Acquisition and Strategic Alliances: Integrating people and cultures.* Oxford, Butterworth-Heinemann.

CASCIO W. F. (1993) 'Downsizing: What do we know? What have we learned?' *Academy of Management Executive.* 7I(1). pp95–104.

EGGERT M. (1991) *Outplacement: A guide to management and delivery.* London, Institute of Personnel Management.

HERZBERG F. (1966) *Work and the Nature of Man.* Cleveland, OH, World Publishing.

HOPSON B. *and* SCALLY M. (1993) *Build Your Own Rainbow.* San Diego, CA, Pfeiffer.

MASLOW A. H. (1971) *The Farther Reaches of Human Nature.* New York, Viking.

SCHWEIGER D. M., IVANCEVICH J. M. *and* POWER F. R. (1987) 'Executive actions for managing human resources before and after acquisition'. *Academy of Management Executive.* 2. pp127–38.

5 EMPLOYEE STRESS

Research has consistently highlighted the link between work experience and employee health and wellbeing (Ganster and Schaubroek, 1991; Schabracq and Cooper, 1997). The costs of occupational stress to organisations is currently extremely high in terms of sickness absence, staff replacement costs, accidents at work and reduced productivity. The CBI estimates that 196 million days were lost in 1998 through sickness (CBI, 1998). According to MIND, the mental health charity, between 30 per cent and 40 per cent of all sickness absence from work is attributable to mental and emotional disturbance. Overall the cost of job stress to industry has been estimated to represent 12 per cent of GNP in the USA and 10 per cent in the UK (Quick, Nelson and Quick, 1990; Cartwright and Cooper, 1996). Occupational stress has increasingly become a significant health and safety issue for UK organisations, as Earnshaw and Cooper (1996) have highlighted in their book on worker compensation and stress-related claims.

One of the fundamental causes of stress is change and its associated uncertainty. Recent surveys (Worrall and Cooper, 1998; 1997) of the membership of the British Institute of Management report that in 1997 59 per cent of respondents had experienced major change in their organisation during the previous year. A follow-up survey in 1998 found that this figure had increased to 62 per cent. The main drivers for change were consistently identified as cost-reduction programmes, redundancies and culture change. In terms of the impact of change, almost 50 per cent of managers considered that morale had become a problem in their organisation and that they had experienced an increased sense of powerlessness in their job.

Mergers and acquisitions are particularly stressful forms of organisational change because they are associated with loss and lack of control and result in change and increased workload. Any loss event requires considerable personal adjustment. Holmes and Rahe (1967) have rated the magnitude of the adjustment to corporate takeover and its associated stress as being equivalent to the gain of a new family member or becoming bankrupt, and more stressful than mortgage foreclosure or the death of a close friend. Cartwright and Cooper (1996) have described the way in which employees respond to merger within the framework of the bereavement model presented in the previous chapter:

Stage 1: disbelief and denial

The individual's first reaction is shock. He or she may deny that the merger or acquisition will ever happen, despite the rumours. Even when the deal goes through, individuals may strive to convince themselves that nothing will change. Often, an existing organisational leader is identified as a champion of the status quo. Hopes are pinned on this champion that he or she will successfully fight to preserve the existing corporate identity and culture and not abandon, compromise or sell-out the company.

If such a person exists, he or she will become very powerful in mobilising resistance to change. Hence the importance (see Chapter 2) of identifying and confronting any hidden agendas which there may be amongst the senior management team from the outset.

Stage 2: anger and resentment

As the reality of the situation becomes more obvious, shock and disbelief are replaced by anger and resentment which may be manifested in overt hostility. Individuals may refuse to co-operate and share information with their new colleagues.

Stage 3: emotional bargaining – from anger to depression

As fear and uncertainty about individual job futures develop, people may become angry with themselves for not anticipating the event and 'bailing out' sooner. They may come to resent the commitment and loyalty they have previously invested. Often, they become nostalgic for the past – indeed, they may even refuse to use the new company name. Feelings of anger may subsequently subside to be replaced by depression.

Stage 4: acceptance

Finally, employees will hopefully recognise that what is past is gone forever and accept the new situation. It may be necessary to move people onto this stage, deliberately injecting a sense of reality by forcing them to consider the harsher consequences that might have occurred if the merger or acquisition had not gone ahead.

Until there is acceptance that any attempt to deny or resist the situation is futile and unproductive, a positive approach will not begin to develop. Becoming stuck at Stages 1, 2 or 3 will result in preoccupied and unproductive behaviour and is likely to be experienced as stressful. Even if people come to accept the situation, they may still feel let down by their old organisation and its management and no longer be as committed to or satisfied with their work or the organisation.

The intensity of the loss experience will vary between individuals depending upon the strength of their attachment to the acquired or merged company. This is likely to hinge upon factors such as age, length of service, organisational commitment, degree of cultural and job satisfaction and position in the organisation, as well as on personality characteristics. Some people will adjust more quickly than others. Some may experience little or no sense of loss at all. This may be because they have experienced and survived a merger before, or felt unappreciated or oppressed by their current organisation and its culture. If the future of the company has been precarious for a long time, it may be that for some the relief of being acquired or merged overpowers any sense of loss.

However, everybody involved in an M&A has to adjust to some degree of change. There are numerous research studies which have highlighted the stress associated with organisational restructuring and its impact on individual and organisational outcomes. In a study of the reorganisation of a US government department (Buono and Bowditch, 1989), stress was shown to have a profoundly negative impact on productivity. One manager estimated that the atmosphere of gloom cost the equivalent of about a month's work per year per employee. Walsh and Tracey (Buono and Bowditch, 1989) found that stress resulting from the reorganisation of another US government office led to an increase in turnover intentions and a significant decrease in job participation, pay satisfaction and intrinsic motivation.

In a longitudinal study in the UK of over 1,500 employees involved in the transition from a public- to private-sector organisation (Nelson, Cooper and Jackson, 1995), it was found that levels of job satisfaction and mental and physical health declined significantly. Furthermore, those in positions of less control and higher uncertainty (ie manual workers) suffered the greatest negative effects of major organisational change.

According to Philip Mirvis (1985), M&As are different from other forms of organisational restructuring in terms of the speed of change, the scale of change and the critical mass of the unknown which they present to both parties and which possibly make them even more stressful. There are relatively few empirical research studies which have specifically investigated merger stress. In a study of over 150 middle managers involved in a large UK building society merger (Cartwright and Cooper, 1992), mental health measurements taken approximately six months post-merger integration showed that more than one third of the managers surveyed recorded mental health scores comparable to, or worse than, the scores of psychoneurotic outpatients. This occurred even though it was a friendly merger between two culturally very similar organisations. The results also indicated that the merger had been significantly more stressful for managers of the smaller merger partner. Another study (Siu, Cooper and Donald, 1997) investigating stress amongst employees of an acquired TV company provides further evidence regarding the negative impact of the change event on employee health, particularly those in middle management positions. Levels of job satisfaction and physical and psychological health were found to be significantly below average. Specifically, high stress levels emanating from relationships with other people and organisational structure and climate were strong predictors of job dissatisfaction, whereas stress associated with the managerial role was a strong predictor of both physical and mental ill health. Fried *et al* (1996) also focused on the impact of corporate acquisition on middle managers. They found that levels of experienced stress were linked to perceptions of the fairness of treatment of terminated employees. In a study of a large manufacturing organisation, the incidence of high blood pressure doubled from 11 per cent in the year prior to acquisition to 22 per cent in the first year post-acquisition (Marks and Mirvis, 1997).

Sources of merger stress

General models of occupational stress (see Figure 2) conceptualise potential sources of stress in the workplace as emanating from six aspects of work-related behaviour and experience.

As major organisational change events, M&As are likely to affect all areas, possibly simultaneously. Importantly, they are events which precipitate change that an individual has not self-selected and is psychologically unprepared for.

The most common stressors associated with M&A have been identified (Cartwright and Cooper, 1996) as being:

- loss of identity
- increased organisational size
- fear of job loss or demotion
- the possibility of job transfer or relocation
- lack of information, poor or inconsistent communication
- loss of or reduced power, status and prestige
- disturbed or uncertain career path
- lack of control and consultation
- changes in rules, regulations, procedures and reporting arrangements
- changes in colleagues, boss and subordinates
- ambiguous reporting systems and unclear roles
- redundancy and devaluation of old skills and expertise
- personality and culture clashes
- increased workload.

In the early stages of the merger or acquisition process, stress will be associated with factors which affect personal survival, ie job loss, relocation. As the merger progresses, this

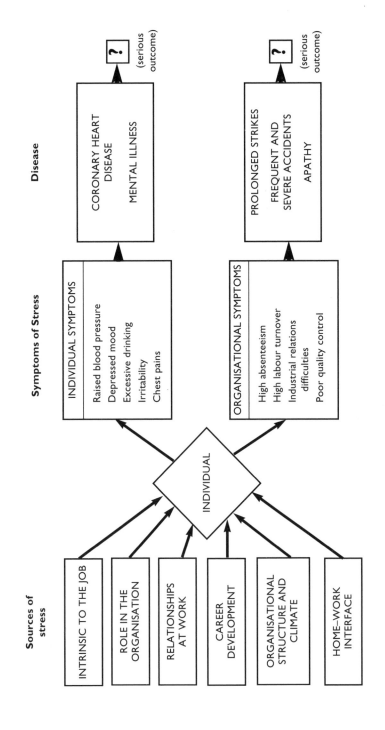

Figure 2
STRESS – A RESEARCH MODEL

Sources of stress

| INTRINSIC TO THE JOB |
| ROLE IN THE ORGANISATION |
| RELATIONSHIPS AT WORK |
| CAREER DEVELOPMENT |
| ORGANISATIONAL STRUCTURE AND CLIMATE |
| HOME-WORK INTERFACE |

INDIVIDUAL

Symptoms of Stress

INDIVIDUAL SYMPTOMS

Raised blood pressure
Depressed mood
Excessive drinking
Irritability
Chest pains

ORGANISATIONAL SYMPTOMS

High absenteeism
High labour turnover
Industrial relations difficulties
Poor quality control

Disease

CORONARY HEART DISEASE

MENTAL ILLNESS

? (serious outcome)

PROLONGED STRIKES

FREQUENT AND SEVERE ACCIDENTS

APATHY

? (serious outcome)

will be replaced by stress associated with changes in work organisation and culture.

The prospect of being taken over as opposed to merging might seem potentially more traumatic, whereas in reality the reverse is true. Mergers differ from acquisitions in a number of ways which make them inherently more stressful. Comparative to acquisitions, mergers result in:

❑ significantly more role duplicity and overlap which is likely to invoke competition and jealousy amongst organisational members

❑ more ambiguous power and cultural dynamics

❑ an unacceptably long period of organisational limbo between the time the merger is announced and the intro-duction of any actual change.

Coping with merger stress

Universally, the most stressful aspects of M&As are fear of job loss and living with uncertainty. Studies have shown such merger stressors to be linked to sleep problems, dizziness and loss of appetite (Greenhalgh and Rosenblatt, 1984). Employees are often reluctant to admit that they have difficulties coping with stress in more normal and less threatening organisational circumstances. However, in M&A situations employees are even more likely to 'bottle up' or disguise any stress they may be experiencing so as not to give any indication that they may not be 'merger-fit'. Indeed, it is not unusual for employees to voluntarily take on extra role tasks or adopt more extrovert behaviour, to convince others of their worth and make sure that they get themselves noticed.

In an anonymous post-merger survey (Cartwright and Cooper, 1992), 78 per cent of employees reported that the merger had caused them some degree of stress; 20 per cent reported that they had coped badly and had not developed any effective strategy for dealing with stress. One of the main strategies which surveyed employees used to combat stress was talking with a spouse or partner. Although the social support of family and friends is an important and useful strategy for coping with stress, because the consequences of M&As may have important family repercussions (eg job loss or relocation), sharing anxieties might serve only to heighten partner stress.

In another study of almost 300 employees examining the way in which individuals coped with merger stress (Cartwright and Hudson, 2000), the findings suggested that employees who tended to adopt a more 'here-and-now' approach and did not think too much about the future coped better than their colleagues. Although generally regarded as a positive coping resource in this study, seeking social support was associated with poorer physical and psychological health. Interestingly, those employees who had previous experience of mergers did not perceive the merger as being any less stressful than those without prior experience – however, they coped better, they perceived themselves to have a higher level of personal influence and their physical and psychological health was significantly less affected by the experience.

Some individuals are more vulnerable to stress than others. A variety of personal factors impact on the way in which an individual appraises a potentially stressful event. These include age, education, gender, past experience, training, personal needs and wants, as well as a variety of personality characteristics, eg extraversion or introversion, neuroticism, tolerance of ambiguity, etc. Individuals who display Type A behaviour tend to perceive stress in a more exaggerated fashion and are particularly prone to stress. Type A behaviour (TAB) or 'hurry sickness' refers to an overall style or manner of behaviour that is characterised by excessive time urgency and consciousness, abruptness of speech and gesture, competitiveness, and a tendency to bottle up anger.

Another important individual moderator of stress is 'locus of control' (Rotter, 1966). Locus of control refers to the extent to which an individual perceives that he or she has control over the events that affect his or her life. Research has shown that we differ in our perceptions of control. Someone with an 'internal locus of control' believes that he or she has control over what happens to them, and that individual decisions and actions which he or she takes influence personal outcomes. The belief that we play a role in determining the events that impinge upon us is considered an important personal resource in coping with stress. Individuals with an 'internalised locus of control' therefore appear to suffer less threat and fewer adverse consequences than more 'externally' controlled people who tend to believe in luck or fate and perceive very little control over things that concern them.

Organisational strategies for tackling the problem of merger stress

In a study of the merger of two Canadian accountancy practices (Greenwood *et al*, 1994) researchers found that less than 10 per cent of employees reported experiencing merger stress. The low incidence of stress was attributed to the careful and sensitive management of personnel issues and the fact that the organisations were culturally compatible.

There are a number of ways in which organisations can act proactively to help reduce merger stress and increase employee perceptions of control. The value of increased communication, consultation and employee involvement has already been discussed. Those with prior merger experience can be a useful resource and source of information to M&A management to encourage individuals to adopt more adaptive methods of coping. However, there are a number of additional ways in which organisations can tackle the problem of merger stress:

- ❏ by conducting stress audits to identify the sources of merger-related stress and to monitor stress and health levels within the organisation throughout the integration process
- ❏ by openly recognising and accepting that stress is a feature of M&As and creating a supportive organisational culture
- ❏ by improving the skills of the workforce to help them cope with experienced stress more effectively through training and educative activities
- ❏ by providing assistance to employees who are experiencing stress.

Stress audits

The most effective way to tackle stress is to take action to modify or eliminate the sources of stress inherent in the M&A situation and so reduce their negative impact on individuals. Some of the stressors (eg job uncertainty) are predictable from the outset, and although they cannot be eliminated their stressful potential can be reduced by providing information. However, there may be some specific organisational, site or departmental stressors operating which may be overlooked or underestimated by the merger management team. In addition, as the merger unfolds a different set of stressors may emerge at different stages in the integration process.

A stress audit provides a means of identifying sources of stress and gaining some indication of existing stress levels and their impact on employee satisfaction and health. Such information is likely to be useful in guiding and directing merger communication strategy, clarifying misinformation and rumour and dispelling unnecessary anxiety. This diagnostic activity will also help the organisation direct its resources into areas where they are most needed. An audit can also provide useful baseline data for monitoring the integration process and its impact on different employee groups.

Stress audits can take the form of a questionnaire survey of all or of a representative sample of the workforce. There are a number of reliable and valid instruments available which have been developed to measure stress levels, sources of stress, employee job satisfaction and physical and psychological health, as well as coping strategies. The Occupational Stress Indicator (OSI) devised by Cooper, Sloan and Williams (1988) and the more recent Pressure Management Indicator (PMI) (Williams and Cooper, 1998) are two examples of such instruments. Many measurement systems require specialist training to administer and interpret. The advantage of such measures is that they can provide the means whereby the organisation can benchmark its results in comparison with those of similar occupational groups. Because of the restrictions on test usage, formal stress audits that use standardised measurements can be rather expensive. When deciding to introduce a stress audit, the HR function must ensure that employees do not perceive it to be a redundancy selection tool. The audit should be completed anonymously, and employees given generic feed-back on the results and the actions which the organisation proposes to take as a result.

Alternatively, there are more informal ways of conducting a stress audit. Sources of stress and dissatisfaction can be collected by setting up a series of small group discussions throughout the organisation, perhaps on a departmental basis. Attendance at such groups should again be voluntary and the sessions should be facilitated by an external third party or a member of the HR team who is trusted by the group. Again, it is important that 'boss' relationships in the group are avoided and that the individual confidentiality of the participants is respected. Some organisations provide work teams with 'scream boards' on which members can record any stressors they have encountered during the day. These are then regularly discussed in team meetings and reported to HR. Another option is to incorporate items relating to stress and health into employee attitude surveys.

It is important that the HRM function remain alert to the more obvious signs of stress within the workforce by closely monitoring sickness absence rates and regularly liaising with the company doctor and health and safety representatives.

Creating a supportive climate

Organisations need to create the kind of supportive organisational climate in which stress is recognised and accepted as a feature of a changing environment and not interpreted as a sign of weakness. Stress-related mental ill health is indiscriminate. Mental illness is as common as heart disease and three times as common as cancer. HRM has an important role to play in raising awareness, and in co-ordinating and implementing an organisation-wide policy to maintain a healthy and productive workforce.

Stress management programmes

Training and information can also be provided to help employees and managers recognise the symptoms of stress in themselves and others and develop some basic stress management skills. Common symptoms of stress are described in Table 3.

Although the form and content of stress management programmes can vary immensely, typically such programmes include training in simple relaxation techniques, lifestyle advice and basic time management and assertiveness skills.

The delivery of such programmes is best undertaken by external experts. However, their success is heavily dependent upon the visible support and commitment of senior management. Alternatively, it may be useful to produce a series of simple fact sheets giving information about stress and stress management, and to make these available to managers and employees.

Table 3
COMMON SYMPTOMS OF STRESS

Physical	palpitations and chest pains indigestion diarrhoea/frequent urination impotence/menstrual problems tingling in arms and legs muscle tension headaches skin rashes visual problems
Behavioural	indecision and unreasonable complaints delayed recovery from illness and accidents accident proneness and careless driving poor work/absenteeism increased smoking/use of alcohol dependence on drugs overeating or loss of appetite sleep problems
Emotional	excessive and rapid mood swings worrying unreasonably about things that do not matter inability to feel sympathy for other people excessive concern about physical health withdrawal and daydreams feelings of tiredness and lack of concentration increased irritability and anxiety

Health enhancement programmes

Evidence (Whatmore, Cartwright and Cooper, 1999) is consistently emerging that regular exercise and improvements in physical fitness play a significant role in developing resilience to stress. As part of the post-merger/acquisition review of organisational policies and practices, an opportunity arises to consider current and future organisational initiatives to promote positive health in the workplace. These may include the introduction of regular medical checks and health screening, 'healthy' canteen menus, and access to keep-fit facilities and exercise classes – or the introduction of cardiovascular fitness programmes, advice on alcohol and dietary control or smoking cessation programmes.

Evidence from health promotion programmes in the USA have produced some impressive results. The New York Telephone Company's Wellness programme designed to improve cardiovascular fitness saved the organisation $2.7 million in absence and treatment costs in one year alone. Similarly, General Motors Corporation report a 40 per cent decrease in lost time and a 60 per cent decrease in accidents and sickness benefits as a result of their programme (Cooper, Cooper and Eaker, 1988).

Good employee health is important to all organisations. However, it is especially significant to recently merged or acquired organisations, when increased workloads are seemingly inevitable.

Counselling services

There has been an enormous growth in the number of UK organisations who provide professional counselling services for employees who are experiencing stress-related problems in the work or personal domain. Such services are provided either by in-house counsellors or by external agencies. The average cost per employee is typically in the region of £25.

The provision of counselling services is likely to be particularly effective in dealing with stress as a result of merger stressors which cannot be changed. If an organisation does not already have in place a counselling service or employee assistance programme, then it may be worthwhile introducing some form of service on a temporary basis to provide support during the early stages of the merger. Surveys on the effectiveness of counselling (Cooper *et al*, 1990; Berridge, Cooper and Highley-Marchington, 1997) have generally found it to be extremely good at improving psychological health, reducing anxiety, improving self-esteem and reducing sickness absence.

In an M&A situation, organisations need to demonstrate their recognition that such experiences can be extremely stressful, temporarily at least, and take steps to ensure that individuals feel they have support. Apart from reducing the negative impact which stress may have on the performance and health of the workforce, some form of intervention programme put in place by the organisation will also positively communicate to employees that it is a caring employer.

References

BERRIDGE J., COOPER C. L. *and* HIGHLEY-MARCHINGTON C. (1997) *Employee Assistance and Workplace Counselling*. Chichester, John Wiley & Sons.

BUONO A. F. *and* BOWDITCH J. L. (1989) *The Human Side of Mergers and Acquisitions*. San Francisco, CA, Jossey-Bass.

CARTWRIGHT S. *and* COOPER C. L. (1993) 'The psychological impact of merger and acquisitions on the individual: a study of building society managers'. *Human Relations*. 46. pp327–47.

CARTWRIGHT S. *and* COOPER C. L. (1996) *Managing Work Place Stress*. London and Thousand Oaks, CA, Sage Publications.

CARTWRIGHT S. *and* HUDSON S. L. (2000) 'Coping with mergers and acquisitions', in R. Burke *and* C. L. Cooper (eds), *Organisation in Crisis: Downsizing, restructuring and privatisation*, Oxford, Blackwell.

COOPER C. L., SADRI G., ALLISON T. *and* REYNOLDS P. (1990) 'Stress counselling in the Post Office'. *Counselling Psychology Quarterly*. 3(1). pp3–19.

COOPER C. L., SLOAN S. *and* WILLIAMS S. (1988) *Occupational Stress Indicators*. Windsor, NFER-Nelson.

COOPER C. L., COOPER R. D. *and* EAKER L. (1988) *Living with Stress*. Harmondsworth, Penguin.

EARNSHAW J. and COOPER C. L. (1996) *Stress and Employer Liability*. London, Institute of Personnel and Development.

FRIED Y., TIEGS R. B., NAUGHTON T. J. and ASHWORTH B. E. (1996) "Managers' reactions to a corporate acquisition: a test of an integrative model'. *Journal of Organisational Behaviour*. 17. pp401–27.

GANSTER D. and SCHAUBROEK J. (1991) 'Work stress and employee health'. *Journal of Management*. 17. pp235–71.

GREENHALGH L. and ROSENBLATT Z. (1984) 'Job insecurity: towards conceptual clarity'. *Academy of Management Review*. 9. pp438–48.

GREENWOOD R., HININGS C. R. and BROWN J. (1994) 'Merging professional service firms'. *Organisational Science*. 5(2). pp239–51.

HOLMES T. H. and RAHE R. H. (1969) 'The social readjustment rating scale'. *Journal of Psychosomatic Research*. 11. pp213–18.

MARKS M. L. and MIRVIS H. (1997) 'Revisiting the merger syndrome: dealing with stress, mergers and acquisitions'. *Mergers and Acquisitions*. 31, 6, 21.

MIRVIS P. H. (1985) 'Negotiations after the sale: the roots and ramifications of conflict in an acquisition'. *Journal of Occupational Behaviour*. 6.

NELSON A., COOPER C. L. and JACKSON P. R. (1993) 'Uncertainty amidst change: the impact of privatisation on employee job satisfaction and wellbeing'. *Journal of Occupational and Organisational Psychology*. 68(1). pp57–73.

QUICK J. C., NELSON D. L. and QUICK J. D. (1990) *Stress and Challenge at the Top: The paradox of the successful executive*. Chichester, John Wiley & Sons.

ROTTER J. B. (1966) 'Generalized expectancies for internal versus external control of reinforcement'. *Psychological Monographs*. 80. No. 609.

SCHABRACQ M. and COOPER C. L. (1997) *Handbook of Work and Health Psychology*. Chichester, John Wiley & Sons.

SIU O. L., COOPER C. L. and DONALD I. (1997) 'Occupational stress, job satisfaction and mental health among employees of an acquired TV company in Hong Kong'. *Stress Medicine*. 13. pp99–107.

WHATMORE L., CARTWRIGHT S. *and* COOPER C. L. (1999) 'Stress interventions in the UK: an evaluation of a stress management programme in the public sector', in M. Kompier *and* C. L. Cooper (eds), *Improving Work, Health and Productivity through Stress Prevention: 14 European cases*. London, Routledge.

WILLIAMS S. *and* COOPER C. L. (1998) 'Measuring occupational stress: development of the pressure management indicator'. *Journal of Occupational Health Psychology*. 3, 4. pp306–21.

WORRALL L. *and* COOPER C. L. (1997, 1998, 1999) *Quality WorkLife Survey*. London, Institute of Management.

6 RETENTION, RELOCATION, RETRAINING AND RENEGOTIATION

Reflecting on the lessons learnt from his involvement in the Glaxo Wellcome merger, John Hulme (1996) identified the importance of understanding and establishing a new psychological contract between employer and employee. On merger and acquisition, everybody is effectively joining a new company and should be provided with the information and fairness of treatment afforded to new entrants. One of the key integration tasks that the HRM function must do is to re-examine current roles and job descriptions, and to produce a new employee handbook. In renegotiating both the explicit and implicit terms of the new employer-employee contract, the HRM function will be confronted with the three Rs: retention, relocation and retraining.

Retention

It is inevitable that people will voluntarily leave acquired or merged organisations. However, it is important that those who make that decision do so because they recognise that they are unwilling or unable to fit into the culture of the new organisation, or because they are aware that they will not be able, or are not prepared, to meet the required performance, even if appropriate training is available.

As well as making decisions on whom to release from the

organisation, an organisation needs to tackle the problem of retaining those individuals it can least afford to lose. This means that key individuals have to be identified and interviewed as early as possible. Those individuals who occupy roles involving extensive contact with clients and customers – eg sales personnel and key account handlers – are particularly vulnerable to poachers. So, too, are individuals with a high level of technical knowledge and system expertise, whose replacement would require a substantial investment in terms of time and training.

Interviews with key individuals should focus on establishing any fears and expectations they may have regarding their continued future with the new organisation and changes in work organisation they anticipate or would like to see happen. Such interviews can also be useful in identifying the factors which motivate the individual, so that the organisation can ensure that they adopt a retention strategy aligned to these motivations. For example, if an individual is motivated by 'status' needs, it may be appropriate to reassign his or her job title. Alternatively if an individual thrives on autonomy, then the organisation can focus on ways of widening his or her responsibility. Although it is not necessarily a good policy to offer retention payments, there may be occasions when this may be appropriate.

Some years ago, Rowntrees sold off their modestly-sized packaging division to a large North American organisation. This came as a major shock to their employees who had come to regard a job with Rowntrees as a job for life. The objective of the acquisition was to increase the efficiency and productivity of the operation, and to enable the acquirer to establish a base in the North of England, rather than to achieve savings through head-count reduction. The acquired workforce was mature, long-serving and loyal to the company. The ability to retain this workforce and reattach their loyalty to the new company was key to the success of the acquisition. To the acquirers' advantage, alternative job opportunities in the immediate area were limited. However, in terms of organisational outcomes, retaining a workforce because it has nowhere else to go is rather different from retaining a workforce because they positively want to be there.

It was clear from the outset that the cultures of the two organisations were very different, and that the acquired employees would need to learn new and potentially 'shocking' ways of doing things. Because the acquirer did not want to lose large numbers of employees before it had the opportunity to assess their talent more fully and discover the extent to which they would fit into the radically different new culture it hoped to create, a decision was made to introduce a form of commitment or loyalty bonus. Employees received this bonus if they remained with the new company for the first six months. The scheme proved effective, in that employees felt more secure about their future. It also provided an incentive for them to commit to a six-month socialisation period in which to learn the new culture. The amount of the loyalty payments each individual was promised was related to their previous length of service. The scheme proved to be a successful retention strategy in that there was no 'post-acquisition drift', even after the loyalty bonus had been earned. Absenteeism rates also fell in the same period by 8 per cent. The recognition that the acquiring company valued and rewarded employee loyalty placed an important role in developing trust and a sense of continuity.

Some people may be key to the organisation not because of the role they occupy but because they are influential and command a great deal of respect from their co-workers. It is important that these individuals are also identified early on, and that their commitment and participation in the merger is engaged.

What typically goes wrong in M&As is that people don't know what they should be doing or how to get things done. As a result, performance deteriorates and things start to fall between the cracks. It is therefore important that clear accountabilities, responsibilities and performance measures are quickly established. This means that the HRM function will need to create new job descriptions and personnel specifications, and establish a skills database for the entire organisation. It may seem an onerous task but, to its advantage, starting from scratch provides the opportunity to introduce the type of system you want rather than requiring you to tinker with an inherited system and its shortcomings.

Many companies initiate this process by asking current job-holders in the two combining organisations to write their own job descriptions and submit these to the HR function with an accompanying internal CV. Because some individuals may be more skilled at this task than others, particularly as concerns the details and presentational quality of such documents, it may be useful to provide some guidelines in this respect. In creating a skills database, internal CVs can be used to assess possibilities for redeployment in other areas of the business and to make fairer comparative assessments which can be supported evidentially in any reselection process. Steps should also be taken to conduct follow-up interviews with all members of staff to clarify their understanding and acceptance of new performance requirements.

'Why don't they sack us all and let us apply for our old jobs?' is a frequent comment made by acquired and merged employees alike. At first, this may seem an odd remark to make, given that job loss is such a major worry. However, it reflects employees' underlying concern that their job abilities are assessed in a fair way. Surprisingly, many organisations already have sophisticated selection systems available to them but do not use them in an M&A situation. Reselection decisions are often hastily made and open to accusations of subjective bias. Particularly at managerial level, problems of role duplicity are often more influenced by political considerations than by issues of individual competence. To convey an impression of 'balanced powersharing', real or illusory, it is not unusual for merged organisations to 'carve up the organisational chart' in such a way that if a top finance job goes to an ex-employee of company A, then a top marketing job will go to an ex-employee of company B, and so on. A more objective and fairer means of resolving the problem is to use assessment centres and selection panels as illustrated in the case-study described in Chapter 2 (pages 21–23).

Relocation

Moving to another region or country is a highly stressful experience at any time in one's career, even if there are positive reasons for doing so. As a result of post-merger restructuring and reorganisation, it may be desirable to persuade key individual job-holders or on-line work teams to move to another geographical area. In the context of many M&As, relocation may be the only alternative to job loss that an organisation can offer its employees.

If it is necessary to relocate individuals to another part of the country, the transition will be easier if those affected are provided with support and specific information regarding local facilities, accommodation and employment opportunities for partners and other family members. One of the major hassles of relocation is buying and selling houses. This can be extremely time-consuming and exhausting, particularly for the female partner who is often the one tasked with the responsibility of finding the home and organising the move. People who are asked to relocate will firstly weigh up the financial implications of a job and house move. They are likely to have concerns about house price differentials and negative equity issues. Even if the job move involves a promotion and attracts a salary increase, the financial rewards may be marginal, and often for the first 12 months after a house move people may find they are financially worse off than before the promotion.

The HRM function can provide assistance by negotiating with senior management over the kinds of financial incentives the company is prepared to offer and the relocation costs it will meet – particularly as regards temporary accommodation prior to house purchase. Such details need to be clearly defined from the outset so that the relocating individuals know exactly what they are entitled to. HRM can also provide resource packs which set out local community information and give the addresses and contact details of estate agents, solicitors, childcare and education providers as well as religious and leisure facilities in the area. If large numbers of people are being relocated to an area, the organisation may be able to negotiate discounted accommodation rates with hotels, local gym or health club membership or preferential fee rates with solicitors.

Organisations also need to recognise that most individuals will move as family units and that support needs to be extended to spouses, particularly in cases of dual career couples and couples with young families. According to research conducted by Ivancevich and Matteson (1980), certain age-groups are more susceptible to relocation stress. They high-light the problem as particularly affecting pre-school children who may experience intense feelings of loss and insecurity, and teenagers to whom peer approval and relationships are so important. The family repercussions of post-merger relocation are illustrated by the following comments made by a building society manager:

> The person who suffered most from the merger is my wife – and my wife has had to cope with the problem of moving into a new house, leaving old friends and settling the children into new schools. She has also had to leave a job she enjoyed. I have been so busy settling into my new job, working long hours, etc, I have tended to leave everything else to her. She's also had to put up with listening to me talking for hours about the merger.

Individuals are likely to feel more positive about moving to a new site and neighbourhood if they are afforded the opportunity to familiarise themselves with the environment before they make a permanent move. The HRM function should encourage site visits and family trips to help individuals establish new social support systems. When Sun Bank acquired an Exeter-based bank, it relocated all its operations to Stevenage. As well as organising a series of personnel exchanges and site visits to Stevenage, Sun Bank facilitated this move by also creating opportunities for its newly-acquired employees to participate in social events with their new Stevenage colleagues. These events also often involved families. When colleagues visited from Exeter, it became a practice supported by senior management for Stevenage personnel to invite them to their homes for the evening rather than leave them to eat alone in an anonymous hotel dining-room. Sun Bank also consulted with their acquired employees to find out whether there were any aspects of their old work environment which they would like to retain in their new offices. As it turned out, employees were very attached to their chairs and it was agreed that these would accompany them to Stevenage!

Similarly, when SmithKline Beecham relocated a significant number of employees based at ex-Beecham sites in Surrey to new facilities at Harlow, they organised regular visits to the new site during its construction period. During this period, site plans and details of the work in progress were prominently displayed in the Surrey offices and helped employees come to terms with the move.

In the case of an international M&A, it may be necessary to relocate individuals to another country, which can be even more difficult. There is a voluminous body of literature – for example, Tung, 1981; Jordan and Cartwright, 1998 – which highlights that outstanding performers in a domestic situation do not necessarily perform so effectively in a different cultural setting. A manager with a direct, straightforward 'tell it like it is' negotiation style is likely to be admired and respected in Australia but regarded as naïve or possibly arrogant in Japan. Careful consideration should therefore be given to the selection process. Although different cultures place different emphasis on the characteristics and behaviour they admire or expect in others, which makes successful performance overseas contingent on the specific culture of the host country, there are certain attributes and competencies which seem to be consistently important across cultures (see Table 4).

Openness to experience

In terms of personality attributes, the trait of openness to experience seems to be a constantly recurring personality variable that is linked to successful performance in an international environment. Individuals who hold rigid views about the 'right' and 'wrong' ways of doing things are unlikely to be sufficiently sensitive to and accepting of differences between people. They are likely to become angry and frustrated with the inability of others to share their view of the world. In order to be rewarded by the challenge of working in another cultural environment, an individual needs to possess a curiosity which is stimulated and intrigued by, rather than intolerant of, uncertainty and ambiguity.

Moderate extraversion

Extroverts are often attracted to the challenge, variety and stimulation – and possibly the glamour – of working overseas. Their gregarious nature and ability and need to strike up relationships with others often intuitively make them strong organisational candidates for an overseas vacancy. However, highly extrovert individuals may have considerable difficulty in adapting to more reserved cultures and lack the sensitivity to modify their expressive behaviour and inherent enthusiasm. Most importantly, unless they are extremely competent in the language of the host country, they may be frustrated and feel isolated by their limited communication skills and inability to maintain and receive the attention of others.

Low neuroticism

Similarly, highly anxious individuals who worry excessively and are easily upset are unlikely to be sufficiently robust to cope well with the challenges of a new cultural environment.

Competencies

Cultural sensitivity, good people skills and the ability to form relationships are acknowledged to be an important competencies for expatriate success. To speak the language of the host country well and to be able to manage stress effectively have also been identified as key competencies for expatriates. Studies which have investigated expatriate stress have highlighted that it is important that individuals are able to create and maintain personal stability zones into which they can withdraw under stress. The term 'stability zone' refers to the psychological space and state of comfort into which an individual can retreat by engaging in activities which enable him or her to 'switch off' the stresses around them. Many of the pastimes and activities an individual would normally do back home to help him or her switch off may be culturally specific and be inappropriate or unavailable when overseas – eg playing rugby, digging the garden or going to the theatre or cinema – whereas individuals who engage in pastimes such as reading, painting, writing or cooking can continue with these activities virtually anywhere.

It is also important to recognise that the individual may also have lost valuable support networks and that social support from colleagues and managers will be more limited. Consideration should also be given to the attributes of the spouse or partner of an expatriate manager.

Those who are relocating overseas will need similar but

Table 4
SUMMARY OF PERSONALITY TRAITS AND COMPETENCIES OF THE EXPATRIATE MANAGER

Personality traits	Competencies
Low neuroticism	Relational ability
Moderate extraversion	Culture sensitivity
High openness to experience	Linguistic skill
	Ability to handle stress

Source: J. Jordan and S. Cartwright, *Leadership and Organisation Development Journal*, 19(2), p94.

more extensive information and support compared to those moving to other parts of the country. In addition, both the job-holder and his or her partner would benefit from some form of cross-cultural training to familiarise them with the specific customs, protocol and practices of the country they are moving to. Employment opportunities for female partners may be extremely restricted in some cultures. Partners as well as job-holders should be offered language training. The British Council, which has a long and extensive experience of overseas postings, recognises the importance of support networks. It provides a telephone counselling service link back to the UK for all its overseas employees. In addition, it will also provide 'face-to-face' counselling if required, either by sending one of its own in-house counsellors out to see the individual in situ or by putting the individual in touch with a local counsellor.

The quality of the information and support provided by the organisation to expatriates is critical. Indeed, research has shown (Jordan, 1999) that expatriate adjustment is significantly influenced by the amount of pre-departure planning and organisational assistance and support expatriate couples and families receive. It is important to ensure that expectations are realistic and are likely to be met. As well as practical information about the host country, individuals asked to relocate overseas will also want to know about taxation, financial planning and their longer-term career prospects.

A recent study (Jordan, 1999) of several hundred managers and their partners who relocated overseas concluded that expatriation is as much a process of adjusting to internal change and transition as a process of cultural adjustment. Even expatriates who were rigorously selected and well prepared for the experience experienced increased stress. Jordan suggests that organisations could do more to psychologically prepare the expatriate by providing a well structured pre-departure training programme including elements devoted to the psychology of change and transition and adaptive and maladaptive coping strategies. Expatriation can involve a variety of changes which may be experienced as stressful:

- ❑ language
- ❑ local management style
- ❑ transport systems
- ❑ weather conditions
- ❑ schools and education system
- ❑ dietary and religious laws and restrictions
- ❑ differences in health service provision
- ❑ differences in the concept of time and pace of life.

Retraining

To achieve the expected performance improvements, increased demands and responsibilities will be placed on employees at all levels and pressure will be exerted to upgrade the quality of existing staff. It will therefore be necessary to undertake a post-merger review of current skills and training provisions, and to conduct a training needs analysis to identify any gaps between the current and future requirements of the new business and the existing skills base. Details of the type and amount of training that employees have already received may be ascertained from the internal CV procedure referred to in the earlier section of this chapter.

Product and systems training are obvious areas in which training is likely to be needed. Training may also be a priority in customer service environments to ensure that those who interact with clients provide information and handle enquiries in a consistent way. In addition to technical training, consideration should be given to the kind of interpersonal skills and developmental training that might help employees to adapt to changes in organisational culture and new methods of working. For example, the widening of job roles may result in new or extended managerial responsibilities. The performance and confidence of job-holders is likely to be enhanced by some form of leadership training. Similarly, changes in culture which require managers to place a greater emphasis on oral rather than written communication of ideas and information may mean that some managers will need to develop better presentational skills.

Training needs and initiatives should not just be considered in the context of managerial roles. Changes in culture which increase individual autonomy and expect employees to assume greater decision-making responsibility are unlikely to work without appropriate training support. Existent theories of situational leadership (Hersey and Blanchard, 1982) emphasise that effective task performance does not rely simply on the leadership abilities and style of the individual manager but is as much dependent upon the willingness and competence of those they lead. This notion of 'follower-readiness' suggests that employees' willingness to perform and assume task responsibilities is linked to two aspects of perceived competence: firstly, whether or not they have sufficient expertise and technical competence to actually do the task; and secondly, whether or not they have the self-confidence and psychological maturity to assume the responsibility, and more importantly feel comfortable about accepting the risk associated with the task. Both these aspects have implications for training needs assessment.

People are often reluctant to assume new or increased responsibilities, not necessarily because they are lazy, want to be difficult or are inherently resistant to change, but because they are afraid that they may get things wrong, look foolish in front of others, or suffer excessive blame for the consequences. In the context of a changing environment it is particularly important to develop and nurture the confidence of employees so that they will be prepared to experiment with new working methods and practices. This may also require some understanding and patience on the part of acquiring managers, particularly if the culture of the acquired organisation has been one which strongly discouraged challenge and autonomy, was very unforgiving of employee mistakes or required even minor decisions to be referred upwards.

International mergers and acquisitions raise issues for basic language and cross-cultural training for individuals at all levels in the organisation who have to liaise with overseas colleagues. These issues will be discussed in some detail in Chapter 8.

Finally, much has been written promoting the concept of the 'learning organisation' (Burgoyne *et al*, 1994) and the conditions which organisations need to create if they wish to become this type of organisation. In M&A situations, the conditions for the learning organisation automatically evolve, in that nobody knows everything and everybody needs to learn something. In this respect this presents a tremendous opportunity, provided that this opportunity for learning is recognised by everybody and that the 'learning environment' is nurtured.

When the Leeds Permanent and the Halifax Building Societies announced their merger in the winter of 1994, the prevailing opinion was that a large number of job losses would inevitably follow. In reality, this proved not to be the case and, as the following case-study illustrates, the organisation rapidly introduced retraining as a means of providing alternative job opportunities in other parts of the business.

Case-study

BIG AND BEAUTIFUL: THE MERGER OF THE HALIFAX AND LEEDS PERMANENT BUILDING SOCIETIES

Following the collapse of the proposed merger with The National and Provincial, the Leeds Permanent reconsidered its strategy and renewed its search for a more compatible merger partner. The Halifax was a logical choice. The company was looking for growth opportunities, the CEO of the Halifax had been at the Leeds, and the cultures of the two organisations were similar in many respects. Negotiations began with a series of small off-site meetings in the summer of 1994,and eventually a deal and a detailed merger plan was agreed. On 25 November 1994, the merger and proposed conversion to a plc was announced in *The Independent*. The announcement was precipitated by a leak to the press by a 'reliable source' and was somewhat premature, for the senior management team had plans in place to make a formal announcement on 12 December. This was an unfortunate start, and as a result over half the staff learnt of the merger by means other than official company channels.

The merger between the Halifax and the Leeds Permanent brought together the largest and the fifth-largest building society in the UK. Its conversion to a plc created the country's third-largest bank. At the time of the merger announcement, the combined assets of the two organisations were in the region of £86 billion, with profits of over £1 billion. By the time of the flotation in June 1997, its assets had risen to £116 billion and it had 20 million customers. In terms of employees, the size of the combined workforce was approximately 28,000 involving several hundred overlapping branches.

A lot of planning had gone into the merger process during the negotiation period and it had been decided that there would be strict adherence to a policy of no compulsory redundancies. This was confirmed in writing to the unions. Employment reductions would be achieved through natural wastage, voluntary redundancy and early retirement. Wherever possible, the problem of role duplications would be addressed by providing retraining opportunities for individuals to move across to jobs in the rapidly expanding insurance business. A Jobs Management Unit was set up to handle these issues. In total 100 people took up offers of early retirement and/or voluntary redundancy. Over a six-week period, 5,000 employees received intensive training and over 20,000 received substantial training. The decision to adopt a no-compulsory-redundancies policy sent a powerful message to merged employees that they were valued by the organisation and that their future was secure. This is most important in our industry because people are the instrument that makes money!

The reaction from the City was somewhat different, and we were regarded as being rather wimpish for not sacking people and following the usual convention in such circumstances. Although it could be argued that we were financially fortunate to be able to afford such a policy, in our opinion merged organisations who depend upon achieving results through cost-reduction strategies will not win out in the long term.

The task we faced was enormous in scale. We had to introduce a merger, integrate our operations and then move on to prepare for the conversion. In preparation for the merger, a senior working party had been set up to brainstorm all the HR issues that we would need to address and communicate about from day 1 onwards – eg company car schemes, salaries and pension arrangements, etc. It was agreed that we would retain the more generous and best features of the policies and practices across the two societies to demonstrate fair play to both employee groups.

We introduced *Converge*, a fortnightly internal newsletter, to inform employees on merger-related issues and to combat disturbing rumours that were appearing in the press. A telephone hot line was set up which was staffed by 230 trained staff. Merger project offices were formed in Halifax and Leeds which comprised staff drawn from both societies. Pilot projects were introduced to assess ways of integrating the business. Staff from the Halifax were seconded to Leeds branches to familiarise them with the different ways of working.

In addressing the problem of corporate identify and branding, external customer research was commissioned. On the basis of the results, the new merged organisation retained the Halifax mission and name and adopted the brand names of most of the Leeds products. Staff were issued with a new uniform which symbolised a new 'people' brand. Reorganisation of the branch network resulted in a reduction from 1,150 to 800 branches. Where there were branch closures, new and bigger combined branch premises were set up.

Employee response and integration progress has been monitored through attitude surveys. Not surprisingly, employees of the Leeds, the smaller merger partner, were more anxious about the merger than their Halifax colleagues. Steps were actively taken to reassure them. In the first six months post-merger, Roger Boyes travelled the country and hosted 25 dinners for local Leeds management and staff at all levels. It was considered most important that we demonstrated the commitment and value we placed on all our staff. When an unexpected but important meeting was called which coincided with a dinner for staff in Southampton, Roger hired a private plane so that he could make both the dinner in Southampton and the important meeting with the Regulators. This was a very important statement to make. The message was simple: Roger considered that the meeting with the staff rated equally with a meeting with the Regulators.

Although the cultures were considered similar, they could never be identical – differences did emerge, and these had to be worked through. The introduction of a new and revitalised staff suggestion scheme helped, and in the first three weeks of its operation, 2,500 suggestions were submitted.

Follow-up attitude surveys conducted one year post-merger found that 73 per cent of the 19,000 employees who participated considered that the organisation had a clear vision, and 60 per cent reported that they had been well informed about the merger. The merger and the subsequent flotation was an exhausting and demanding time for everybody – but from strength comes security.

Source: Roger Boyes, Group finance director, and Mike Blackburn, chief executive officer, Halifax Building Society

Renegotiation

As has been discussed, M&As effectively terminate the existing psychological contract between employer and employee and a new contract has to be established. Rousseau (1990) discusses the concept of the psychological contract in terms of two distinct sets of reciprocal obligations between employer and employee which she describes as *relational* and *transactional*. Central to relational contracts is the notion that the relationship between two parties is potentially long-term and is founded on the premise that the employee has obligations to be loyal to the company, and in turn the employer is obliged to provide job security. Factors such as recognition, training, fairness and justice of treatment, as well as support with problems, reinforce the existence and continuance of a relational contract. In contrast, in transactional contracts the reciprocal obligations between employee and employer are founded on economic exchange and perceptions of equity. In other words, the employee is obliged to work hard and the employer has obligations to reward the employee commensurately. According to Rousseau, relational contracts invoke higher levels of commitment than transactional contracts.

When an organisation is acquired or merged, employees are likely to perceive that any relational contract has been violated. The attachment between employer and employee therefore depends upon the strength and adequacy of the transactional contract between the two – hence the immediate preoccupation of employees with factors relating to reward and performance. These obviously constitute a priority issue and were the focus of the previous chapter. However, this should not detract from the deeper and less superficial factors such as recognition, training and support which will re-establish that relational contract and build commitment.

A consistent theme of many of the recent mergers and acquisitions featured in this book has been the importance of communicating to employees that they are valued, and that they will be supported in their endeavours to try out new ways of doing things and to adjust to a new culture. The chief executive of AstraZeneca, Tom McKillop (see Chapter 3), in his statement to employees expressed his intention to build a new organisation that was 'fast, fair, flexible and *forgiving*', thus emphasising that the organisation recognises it is only through change and experimentation with new ideas and methods that one moves forward – and, more importantly, that change will not happen if people are afraid of the consequences of getting things wrong. Similarly, a strong message embodied in the Pathway to Excellence change programme introduced by Aon Risk Services (see Chapter 7) is that 'It's okay to make a mistake.'

References

BURGOYNE J., PEDLER M. *and* BOYDELL T. (1994) *Towards the Learning Company*. Maidenhead, McGraw-Hill.

HERSEY P. *and* BLANCHARD K. H. (1982) *The Management of Organisational Behaviour: Utilizing human resources*. Englewood Cliffs, Prentice Hall.

HULME J. (1996) 'Maintaining business and individuals' performance during the world's largest pharmaceutical merger'. Presentation at Mergers and Acquisitions: The human impact. International Communication for Management Conference, Selfridges Hotel, London, January.

IVANCEVICH J. M. *and* MATTESON M. T. (1980) *Stress at Work*. Glenview, IL, Scott Foresman.

JORDAN J. (1999) 'An exploration of expatriate stress and coping'. Unpublished PhD dissertation, UMIST.

JORDAN J. *and* CARTWRIGHT S. (1998) 'Selecting expatriate managers: a review'. *Leadership and Organisational*

Development Journal. 19(2). pp89–97.

Rousseau D. M. (1990) 'New hire perceptions of their own and their employer's obligations: a study of psychological contracts'. *Journal of Organisational Behaviour.* 11. pp389–400.

Tung R. (1981) 'The selecting and training of personnel for overseas assignments'. *Columbia Journal of World Business.* 16. pp68–78.

7 GETTING DOWN TO INTEGRATION: FROM 'WE v THEM' TO 'US'

The problem of integrating two, often previously rival, work-forces and their cultures and getting them to co-operate and work together cannot be underestimated. There is always an inherent danger that the acquiring or dominant merger partner will destroy the very attributes that caused it to want to buy into the other company in the first place. Many innovative companies have found their creative potential and entrepre-neurial spirit stifled by the bureaucracy and constraints placed upon it when an acquiring company has moved to assimilate its operations and bring it into line with mainstream corporate policies and practices.

M&As to some degree involve integration at three levels – physical, systems-procedural and socio-cultural. Fear of change amongst the workforces of both combining organisations invariably leads to a protective closing of ranks. This increased cohesiveness occurs whether or not the takeover or merger is considered to be friendly or hostile, and regardless of whether or not individuals see it as a threat or an opportunity. Characteristically, employees focus on the differences rather than any similarities in corporate cultures and see each other as competitors, reckoning that gains on one side will be matched by losses to the other. A 'we' versus 'them' mentality develops and territorial battles ensue over a range of major and – more frequently – minor issues. In an acquisition, power is substantially assumed by the new parent and the buyer will assert its culture of 'superiority' by bringing about change as quickly as possible, imposing its own control systems and financial restraints. Organisations involved in a merger, however, tend to continue as separate entities for some time after the merger, and the 'we v them' mentality becomes more firmly entrenched.

This has implications for the individuals involved. It means that during an acquisition there is likely to be more obvious conflict and resistance, mixed with feelings of powerlessness. The prevailing attitude becomes one of 'Just because their way of doing things worked for them doesn't mean it'll work for us.' However, the more prolonged nature of a merger means that the individuals involved can be disrupted by uncertainty for a much longer period, leading to its own set of problems.

Physical integration

Some years ago, a number of studies were conducted examining the development of interpersonal relationships and friendship patterns in residential housing projects (Nahemow and Lawton, 1975). Such studies consistently showed that people were more likely to form relationships with their near neighbours, people whom they passed on the street or in the hall of their apartment building on a regular basis. Physical proximity and the informal day-to-day contact which results is an important determinant in bonding people together. Indeed, an important aspect of building an effective team is ensuring that they have the opportunity to spend time in close physical proximity with each other.

In the context of M&As, as has been discussed, it is important that opportunities are created for the combining employee groups to interact and become acquainted with each other as early as possible, in both a work and social context. However, it is also important, in the early stages at least, to avoid creating situations which will promote rivalries and comparative evaluations – eg inter-office football matches.

The physical working environment plays an important part in shaping and reinforcing existing cultural values, norms and ways of behaving. Pre-existing corporate identities and cultures will continue to be maintained if organisational members remain in an unchanged physical working environment. Some staff movements and changes in the physical layout, decoration and 'feel' of the working environment will help the development of a new corporate identity and culture. The site which becomes the corporate headquarters, as the perceived seat of power, is extremely symbolic. If the 'new' corporate headquarters seems little different in ambience and staffing arrangements from the way it was as the former HQ of one of the merger partners, this will perpetuate its identity, legacy culture and superiority in terms of power. From the outset, organisations need to identify their integration priorities in areas, functions and employee groups. For most organisations, the main priorities will lie in the integration of the sales force and the bringing together of the top management team, and are most critical. Although it may be a costly option, moving people to a brand new location is arguably one of the most effective ways of creating a new and different organisational culture.

Systems-procedural integration

Similarly, priorities need to be set regarding systems-procedural integration. The capabilities of existing systems, and more importantly, the future requirements, have to be carefully assessed and reviewed. This is best achieved through the formation of joint task groups or working parties in consultation with end users.

Socio-cultural integration

Culture, in that it provides organisations with stability, order and cohesion, is not really meant to change. Bate (1990) has suggested that organisations can easily become prisoners of their own culture and find it difficult to reverse or change the direction of the pattern of learned behaviours. For example, organisations tend towards more extreme forms of their existing culture so that role cultures will predominantly tend to become more obviously bureaucratic over time. There are a number of forces against change inherent in individuals and organisations.

On the part of individuals	On the part of organisations
Fear of failure	Organisational leaders
Loss of status	Strength of culture
Inertia (habit)	Rigidity of structure
Fear of the unknown	Sunk costs
Loss of friends	Lack of resources
	Contractual agreements
	Strongly held beliefs and recipes for evaluating corporate activities

At the deepest implicit level, culture is thought of as a complex set of values, beliefs and assumptions that define the way in which an organisation goes about its business. Such core beliefs and assumptions are manifested in the structures, symbols, myths, rituals and practices which form the explicit culture of the organisations. It may be rather easier therefore to adjust the manifestations of the culture than it is to change the core beliefs and assumptions within an organisation. In the context of cultural integration, any practical strategy for change has to involve thought and action at both implicit and explicit levels. According to Buchowicz (1990) 'Any decision to radically change, integrate or maintain an existing culture firstly requires an understanding of the cultural and subcultural values throughout the organisation.'

Defining the starting-point

As discussed in Chapter 2, some impressions of the culture of the combining organisations will have been gained at the negotiation stage. There are many frameworks that can be used to understand and describe culture. Roger Harrison (1972) has suggested that organisational culture can be conceptualised as falling into any one of four broad or ideal types, namely power, role, task/achievement and person/support cultures.

Power culture

This is often found in small entrepreneur-led and family firms. Larger organisations with a strong figurehead and/or a long history and respect for tradition can also be power cultures. Centralised decision-making is the main feature of a power culture, which makes it flexible and swift to react. Restricted information is provided to employees on a 'need-to-know' basis; communication structures and the flow of information is usually of a top-down nature, and the management style is one of command and control.

The relationship between management and staff is often akin to that between parent and child. This may manifest itself in a benevolent, caring and paternalistic attitude towards employees, or alternatively it may be experienced as autocratic, controlling and critical. Power cultures are often built around employee loyalty to the organisational leader(s) and demand that employees are complaint-oriented rather than challenging and participative.

Role culture

A role culture is typified by logic, rationality and the achievement of maximum efficiency. Bureaucracy is the norm and the company 'bible' rules. Roles are often specialised and well-defined, making the role more important than the people or personalities that occupy them. This type of culture is hierarchical in structure; competition between departments is common; employees are very status-conscious and there are often many status symbols in evidence. Moving up the organisation invariably means moving to a bigger and better-fitted office and driving a larger and more luxurious company car. Role cultures function well in stable environments but are slow to change. They tend to hamper innovation and are often experienced by their members as being frustrating and impersonal.

Task/achievement culture

In this type of culture *what* has been achieved tends to be more important than *how* it was achieved. Task cultures focus on securing the necessary resources and skills to deliver what is required. This type of culture often exists in creative industries such as advertising and media or as a departmental subculture in parts of an organisation – eg research and development. It is a team culture which values expertise and task commitment. Often described as 'marching to its own drum', it is sometimes accused of giving the customer what it (the company) thinks is right rather than what the customer wants. Task cultures tend to be experienced as stimulating, but they are also exhausting and demanding cultures in which to work, and problems of burn-out are not uncommon.

Person/support culture

Egalitarianism is the key value in this type of culture. Person/support cultures adopt the notion that the organisation exists to advance the personal growth and development of its members. Structure is minimal, and information, influence and decision-making are shared equally. It is most often found operating in communities and co-operatives, although there may be strong elements of a person/support culture operating in some profit-making organisations.

Cultures which are essentially of a similar type tend to integrate more easily. However the integration of two power cultures can be problematic and lead to personality clashes and power struggles at the top. In such circumstances, success often depends upon the acceptability of the new emergent leader and the extent to which he or she is able to reattach employee loyalty to any former displaced leader.

As a starting-point it can be useful to think of organisational culture within this framework and to assess the degree of cultural compatibility between organisations on the basis of initial cultural impressions. However, culture is to an organisation what personality is to the individual. Individuals, like organisations, can be categorised in broad types – eg extroverts and introverts. While such categories provide a cognitively simple and meaningful way of differentiating between individuals, they do not provide a sufficiently detailed insight into the inevitable differences which exist between individuals whom we might broadly classify as being extrovert to the extent that we can understand and possibly predict all aspects of their behaviour and the underlying personal values which drive that behaviour. In the case of organisations there is the additional problem that the outwardly presented or espoused culture may be somewhat different from the subcultures and dominant 'culture-in-use' in the organisation.

It is therefore important that steps are taken to more fully understand and explore the cultures of the combining organisations at all employee levels in the early post-acquisition/merger period. Such information could be collected through focus group discussions and/or questionnaires. Increased objectivity might be gained by using a third party/consultant to do this.

As a checklist of items to be explored in employee discussions, the following guidelines are suggested:

❏ What things about this (your current) organisation (ie values, systems, practices, managerial style, etc) would you *not* like to see changed?

❏ What things about this (your current) organisation would you *like* to see changed or maybe even in the past have tried to change without success?

❏ What makes a 'good employee' in this organisation?

❏ What makes a good manager/boss in this organisation?

❏ What are the main areas in which the organisation could improve/do things better?

❏ What do you *actually* know about the acquiring organisation or other merger partner? What would you *like* to know?

❏ What do you expect will change?

❏ What do you *hope* will change?

There are a number of culture questionnaires which have been developed (Cooke and Lafferty, 1989; Saville and Holdsworth, 1993; Trompenaars, 1993), although there may be restrictions on use. Routinely, the content of such questionnaires includes items relating to the following dimensions of organisational activity of behaviour:

❏ decision-making style

❏ reward mechanisms

❏ good 'citizenship' behaviours

❏ communication structures and systems

❏ customer orientation

❏ attitudes towards risk-taking

❏ employee autonomy.

Questionnaires have the advantage of providing a means of measuring the cultural distance between the combining organisations and a baseline standard against which to monitor change post-integration. They are invariably a more cost-effective/less labour-intensive way of collecting data than qualitative methods. However, to their disadvantage questionnaires in isolation tend to more adequately explain *how* and in what way cultures are different rather than *why* they are different. In other words, they are more useful in tapping into behaviour than uncovering core values and assumptions.

A deeper understanding of the core values of a culture and the mind-set of its members is likely to be achieved through group discussions and observations. Research into M&As (Cartwright, 1998) has stressed the importance of employee involvement and participation in the merger process as a means of reducing uncertainty and feelings of powerlessness, and discussion groups are a particularly useful strategy in actively engaging employee involvement.

Agreeing and committing to new cultural values and behaviours

Unless there is a genuine understanding and cultural exchange between the parties to a merger or acquisition, there is little likelihood that the cultures will integrate effectively. On the basis of the information that each organisation has about itself and the other, the senior management team need to agree upon the vision and the culture of the new organisation they wish to achieve, which reflects and accommodates the views and aspirations of the wider organisational membership.

In defining and communicating these values, the senior management team need to be clear as to the way in which these values will be translated into *actual* behaviours. For example, if the organisation values openness and honesty, how will it demonstrate this at an organisational level, at a managerial level to employees, and what are the reciprocal expectations? A list of values is relatively easy to generate – the difficulty is identifying, agreeing and modelling the supporting behaviours to the extent that they engage and are adopted by the critical mass of people within the organisation.

The following case-study is illustrative of an approach to culture change in which employee involvement and consultation was central to the developing of a new post-merger culture.

Case-study

INVOLVEMENT WORKS – THE DEVELOPMENT OF CHANGE CHAMPIONS: AON RISK SERVICES UK

Traditionally, a merger is conceptualised as involving the integration of two organisations. However, the formation of Aon Risk Services UK in 1997 was rather different and brought together four retail insurance broking and risk management companies: Aon Risk Services UK, Alexander and Alexander, Bain Hogg, and Minet. Aon is a large US multinational company. At the time of the mergers its UK operations were relatively small, employing approximately 500 people. In response to increasing consolidation in this business sector and a recognised need to expand its UK presence, Aon embarked upon a growth strategy through merger and acquisition.

In late 1996/early 1997 Aon completed two merger deals, one with Alexander and Alexander (A&A), which had 1,500 UK employees in their retail operations, and the other with Bain Hogg, which had a slightly larger workforce of 1,800. Whereas Bain Hogg had been through a series of M&As over the previous ten years, in contrast A&A had remained untouched by this type of activity and was new to the merger experience. In September 1997 Aon Risk Services subsequently acquired Minet's with a workforce of around 1,000 employees.

Most of the senior management team of the newly-formed company were drawn from A&A. The culture of A&A was very different from the other partnering organisations, particularly in its emphasis on centralised decision-making. The pace of integration was fast, and expedient measures were taken to quickly integrate the organisations together. A significant number of people were made redundant and we were aware that the morale of our employees had been negatively affected.

Changes in the senior management team were introduced, including the appointment of a new CEO and director. The new management team recognised that while significant progress in terms of physical and procedural integration had taken place, little headway had been made in achieving socio-cultural integration. There remained great divisions in the organisation and employees still clung on to the cultural identity and values of their legacy companies. It was therefore important to stop people talking about the past and to create a shared vision for the future.

Between February and May 1998, a major organisational review was undertaken which centred around providing strategic direction to the business. While it is the role of senior management to lay out the proposed pathway for the future, the wider involvement and commitment of all organisational members is required to ensure that the business successfully moves in the desired direction. In May 1998 the Pathway to Excellence change initiative was launched at the directors' conference. Having outlined the future plans for the business, a major feature of the initiative was to provide everybody with the opportunity to tell senior management what they wanted from the company. Opportunities for employee participation were to be provided through a programme of interviews, focus group discussions and questionnaire surveys.

As part of the initiative, the organisation conducted the 'Your Opinion Counts' survey which achieved a 51 per cent response rate. This, together with data collected from focus group discussions, identified a range of key HR issues and concerns amongst employees including lack of brand awareness, poor communication, lack of reward and recognition, inadequacy of IT and lack of trust. Aon Risk Services responded systematically to these issues in a variety of ways through:

❏ the formation of a series of task groups to investigate current benefit and reward programmes and to make recommendations

❏ investment in IT systems which extended to include PC access for everyone

❏ the establishment of resource centres to co-ordinate the activities and client opportunities that exist across all parts of the business

❏ the introduction of a series of trade fairs to provide employees with the opportunity to meet representatives from other business units and sister companies

❏ dovetailing with other global initiatives which were addressing the issue of increasing brand awareness

❏ increasing employee access to senior management through the establishment of the discussion and executive exchange forums, a means by which employees can e-mail questions and suggestions directly to the chief executive and other senior managers.

A significant theme of the Pathway to Excellence programme was the development of a cohesive organisational culture and the creation of a shared vision and language. In October 1998 Aon carried out a snapshot survey of the leadership behaviour that people would like leaders to adopt and the type of organisation employees would like Aon Risk Services to become. Nearly 2,000 employees responded to the survey and the views expressed formed the core values and mission statement of the organisation. These continue to be prominently communicated and reinforced through-out Aon through posters, screen savers, etc.

Another part of the Pathway to Excellence initiative is an organi-sation-wide training programme called Play to Win. This is provided by a sister company, Pecos River Change Management Group, and is of two- or three-day duration. It incorporates elements of outdoor/adventure type activities and emotional intelligence training.

The aim of the programme is to provide individuals with life skills to help them initiate and cope with change, improve teamworking and develop support networks within the organisation. By December 1999 about 2,000 individuals out of the current workforce had been through the programme, beginning with the top tier of management. It is anticipated that by the end of March 2000 everybody will have had the opportunity to attend a course.

Enthusiasm for the course has provided approximately 250 'change champions' who have returned to the organisation to lead change project groups and to assume support and mentoring roles.

So how successful has all this been in creating an integrated and cohesive organisation? At present, there is a project team conduct-ing an evaluation study on the effectiveness and success of the Play to Win programme and planning another for the future. At the indi-vidual level, feedback from participants has been extremely positive and widespread. The second annual employee opinion survey was conducted in May 1999. The results, based on a 50 per cent response rate, showed an all-round improvement of 5 per cent across all dimensions. Perhaps most encouraging has been the unsolicited feed-back Aon has received from its clients and suppliers who have positively noticed and commented upon the differences in the way we go about our business, and the improvements in our teamworking. Indeed, the Play to Win programme has been introduced into other organisations with whom we deal.

Achieving integration in a merger of this kind has not been easy. We didn't get everything right first time. On reflection, we should have sorted out the employment terms and conditions more quickly. Ideally, we should have completed the Play to Win programme in a shorter time to avoid creating divisions between those who had completed the experience and those who hadn't.

In terms of what we have learnt in the context of future acquisitions, there are a number of pointers to share:

❑ Stay focused on clients.

❑ When we acquire companies in the UK, we try to avoid hostile situations.

❑ Work hard at communicating a shared vision and creating enthusiasm.

❑ Try to secure quick gains – early success.

❑ Exceed legal requirements in terms of consultation and TUPE legislation and provide good support for employees and those who become casualties of the change process.

❑ Work toward making continued employment a first priority – retrain, relocate wherever possible.

❑ Provide employees with the opportunity to be heard, to challenge and to acquire the skills to cope with and create change.

❑ Always remember that acquired or merged employees didn't choose to join you, and that it is your task to demonstrate that you can offer them something better than they had before.

❑ Embrace and support employees willing to challenge the status quo.

❑ Value creativity.

❑ Remove internal barriers.

The Play to Win programme is based around a book by W. Wilson and H. Wilson (1998) *Play to Win: Choosing growth over fear in work and life*: Austin, Texas, Bard Press Inc.

Source: Paul Hodder, HRM director, and Mike Eve, chief executive, Aon Risk Services UK

Transition teams and task-forces

Employee consultation and involvement forms the basic building-block on which to create a new and cohesive culture. This is best achieved by establishing joint working parties at all levels to exchange and establish best practice and as a means of bringing dissenting groups together. The approach of Aon Risk Services typifies this kind of integration strategy. By identifying a common superordinate goal and involving both employee groups in a joint initiative to achieve that goal, employees will begin to focus on the future rather than dwell on what was before. It is particularly important that, as role models, the top management team are seen to be working together and not pulling in different directions. It is the task of top management to communicate a clear direction for the future, demonstrate that it has not taken its eye off the ball and focus the workforce on its external goals. Early wins and successes should be celebrated and widely communicated to reassure organisational members that the changes that have occurred are working and are beneficial.

Promoting cultural change

It is generally accepted that there are four possible approaches to culture change:

- ❏ *Aggressive*: ie telling people to change or else! This approach relies on the use of formal authority to apply pressure to individuals to behave in the required way and being prepared to take punitive action if they do not.
- ❏ *Conciliatory*: ie persuading people to change by sensitive and rational appeal. This approach relies on the use of information, data and logical argument to convince people that it is in their and the organisation's best interest to change their attitudes and behaviour.
- ❏ *Corrosive*: ie eroding resistance to change through informal means. This approach is less direct and involves identifying key individuals at all levels in the organisation who are perceived as influential, enlisting their support and involving them in integration activities.
- ❏ *Indoctrinative or educative*: ie the techniques of the train-

ing room. This approach involves designing and delivering a change programme to a critical mass of people in the organisation which promotes and demonstrates the new values and behaviours. Again, the Play to Win programme which formed part of Aon's change strategy exemplifies this approach.

To be effective, any change strategy has to be prepared to combine elements of all four approaches. Unfortunately, many acquirers rely exclusively on an aggressive 'buy in or buy out' approach, whereas it should be a strategy of last resort when other approaches have failed. Organisations which rely on power-coercion strategies to effect change tend to achieve behavioural compliance rather than the long-term internalisation of new values and attitudes.

Research has shown that the most effective influence strategy is to present individuals with an appeal which is based on rational and logical argument. This means explaining the reason an organisational culture has to change. It may be in response to external forces – ie the social, economic, political and competitive environment in which the company operates. It may be driven by inner forces, such as the organisation's structure, culture and internal politics. In the case of M&A, change is likely to be the necessary outcome of both internal and external drivers.

Whereas the conciliative approach emphasises the importance of communication, individuals may need to develop and practice new skills and behaviours in a 'safe' environment, hence the necessity to incorporate an educative approach. If respected colleagues are seen to actively embrace and support the changes, through their influence they will convince others.

Resistance to change is inevitable. It should not be regarded as undesirable because it is a means of establishing what people value. The important issue is to give individuals the opportunity to voice their resistance. Overt resistance can be confronted and addressed: it is covert resistance that is much more dangerous.

Factors that promote culture change

In summary, there are a variety of factors which promote culture change, the main ones being:

- ❏ recognition (the why and the what) that the culture has to change and an understanding of the direction of culture change
- ❏ reward systems (that reinforce new values and behaviours and which discourage 'deviant' behaviour)
- ❏ changes in the physical environment
- ❏ influx of 'new blood'
- ❏ role models at all levels
- ❏ training
- ❏ participation and consultation in the change process
- ❏ confidence in management/change agents
- ❏ mechanisms for monitoring change
- ❏ clear links between desired change and performance
- ❏ reducing individuals' perception of risk – developing and supporting a 'learning culture'.

References

BATE S. P. (1990) 'A description, evaluation and integration of four approaches to the management of cultural change in organisations'. Paper presented to the Fourth British Academy of Management Conference, Glasgow.

BUCHOWICZ B. S. (1990) 'Cultural transition and attitude change'. *Journal of General Management*. 15(4). pp45–55.

CARTWRIGHT S. (1998) 'Mergers and acquisitions: the case for an organisational marriage counsellor'. *Journal of Professional HRM*. 13. October. pp10–16.

COOKE R. A. *and* LAFFERTY J. C. (1989) *Organisational Culture Inventory*. Plymouth, MI, Human Synergistics.

HARRISON R. (1972) 'How to describe your organisation's character'. *Harvard Business Review*. 5(1). pp119–28.

NAHEMOW L. *and* LAWTON M. P. (1975) 'Similarity and propinquity in friendship formation'. *Journal of Personality and Social Psychology*. 32. pp205–13.

SAVILLE P. *and* HOLDSWORTH R. F. (1993) *Corporate Culture Questionnaire*. Thames Ditton, Surrey.

TROMPENAARS F. (1993) *Riding the Waves of Culture: Understanding cultural diversity in business*. London, Nicholas Brealey.

8 INTEGRATING ACROSS NATIONAL CULTURES

Cross-border acquisitions and mergers account for almost a quarter of M&A activity (ISR, 1999). Multinational organisations can gain competitive advantage by achieving significant worldwide economies of scale, and by capitalising on multiple sources of organisational learning and innovation. However, to be successful they need to have a common strategic direction and possess a mind-set which is cosmopolitan rather than xenophobic (ISR, 1999).

The issue of cultural compatibility and its implications for subsequent integration is important in the context of any interorganisational combination. Cultural differences and the concept of cultural distance can inhibit and positively obstruct management's attempts to integrate and create a coherent and cohesive organisational entity. The problem of cultural integration can be more acute in domestic M&As because they invariably involve a greater degree of physical and procedural integration of their membership than cross-border M&As. However, in order to be successful, international M&As also require certain groups of key individuals to work closely together, at least minimally, to establish a shared understanding of common objectives and strategy.

Researchers in this area (Attendorf, 1986; Cartwright and Cooper 1996) have observed that the first thing organisational members do in an M&A situation is to make assessments and draw conclusions about the 'other culture'. Comparisons of similarities and differences can be based on direct experience, rumour, second-hand reporting and implicit theories and inference. When the partnering organisation is also 'foreign', assessment of the 'other culture' is likely to involve reference to national cultural stereotypes and ideologies. Whereas foreign investment is often welcomed in the countries of Eastern Europe, because it aids economic growth and development, this is not necessarily the case in the more developed economies of Western Europe and the USA, which may be less keen to see national companies pass into the hands of 'foreign' owners. For example, in the 1980s, in response to increasing inward foreign investment into the USA, a number of political action groups (such as the 'Coalition to Stop the Raid on America') were formed to campaign for tighter regulation of M&A activity. Indeed, Olie (1990) has noted that the perceived threat of concentration and nationalism is a barrier to international M&A. One of the characteristics of culture is that it creates a form of ethnocentrism in which one tends to regard activities that do not conform to one's own view of doing business as abnormal and deviant.

Managerial preferences in international M&A partners

Cartwright, Cooper and Jordan (1998) conducted an interesting research study to establish whether different national managerial groups had similar or dissimilar attitudinal preferences towards foreign M&A partners. The study involved several hundred well-travelled international managers with a knowledge of foreign business cultures and who worked for organisations that had been, and expected to continue to be, engaged in cross-border M&A activity. The managers surveyed represented 17 different nationalities, mainly from northern Europe.

The main findings are summarised in Table 5, which shows the highest-ranking 'preference dimension'.

Although both the French and German managers effectively preferred themselves, such a choice was actually found to be legitimate in terms of the questions asked, in that the managers sampled all worked for 'foreign'-owned organisations.

Interestingly, all groups rated the Japanese managerial style as the least compatible with their own, yet it was highly admired in terms of the way in which it conducts its business

Table 5
INTERNATIONAL PREFERENCE DIMENSION

Nationality	No. of managers	1st preference	Rationale
British	262	USA	Positive attitude
French	34	France	Know where you stand
German	58	Germany	Market access
US	19	UK	Professional approach
Dutch	17	Germany/USA	Professional approach/ Market access
Swedish	34	USA	Professional approach
Danish	18	UK	Positive attitude

Source: Cartwright, Cooper and Jordan, 1998

Table 6
LEAST PREFERRED MERGER PARTNER OR ACQUIRER

Nationality	No. of managers	Least preference	Rationale
British	262	Japan	Incompatibility of language
French	34	Japan	Incompatibility through lack of understanding; no shared view of the world
German	58	Japan	Incompatibility through lack of understanding; no shared view of the world
US	19	Japan	Incompatibility of language
Dutch	17	Spain	Incompatibility through lack of understanding
Swedish	34	Italy	'Never know where you stand'/ Incompatibility of language
Danish	18	Italy	Incompatibility of language

Source: Cartwright, Cooper and Jordan, 1998

activities. Overall, Germany was the most admired country in terms of its managerial style, with the USA ranked in second place, on the grounds that both cultures have a positive make-it-happen style characterised by clear decision-making.

It is reasonable to conclude that cross-border M&A decisions are influenced by managerial preferences regarding perceived compatibility of business cultures and managerial styles. The rationale underpinning those choices will reflect both elements of direct experience with other business cultures and stereotypical judgements. Indeed, the findings of this study are in part reflected in current trends in cross-border M&A activity (Mergers and Acquisitions International, 1994).

It is also interesting that although Japanese organisations are much admired by their northern European competitors, they are regarded as the least attractive merger partner.

Traditionally, the standard Anglo-American approach to M&As tends to require the other merger partner or acquired company to assimilate and adopt its culture. A perception of 'the desire to dominate', as sensed by the managers who participated in this research to be characteristic of the Japanese management style, suggests an inherent resistance to accepting the type of cultural imposition inherent in M&A situations. This may partly explain why the Japanese regard M&As as a potentially 'dishonourable' activity, preferring the option of strategic alliances. Indeed, the Japanese word for 'acquisition', *nottori*, also means 'plotted takeover', 'coup'.

Differences in national cultures

Some years ago, Geert Hofstede (1980) conducted a large-scale international study of IBM employees to investigate cultural differences across 53 countries or regions in which IBM operates. The findings of this study still remain influential and provide a useful way of conceptualising differences in national cultures. According to Hofstede there are four important dimensions to culture:

❑ power distance
❑ uncertainty avoidance

- ❏ individualism *v* collectivism

- ❏ masculinity *v* femininity.

Power distance

This dimension refers to the distance between individuals at different levels of a hierarchy. Cultures characterised by high power distance have distinct 'pecking orders' and are accepting of authoritarian attitudes. Examples of high power distance cultures include those of countries such as France, India, Malaysia, Singapore, Mexico and the Arab nations.

Low power distance cultures are those that actively try to narrow the power distances between members and afford the individual worker more opportunity to participate in organisational processes. Low power distance cultures are typified by those of the countries of Scandinavia, the USA, Israel, Canada and the UK.

Uncertainty avoidance

This dimension concerns the extent to which different cultures are tolerant of uncertainty and can accept ambiguity. Cultures which reflect high uncertainty avoidance tend to fear failures, take fewer risks and are change-resistant. Such cultures include those of Greece, Portugal, Japan and the Arab countries. In contrast, low uncertainty avoidance cultures tend to be entrepreneurial and include those of countries like Singapore, Hong Kong, Denmark and the UK.

Individualism v collectivism

Individualist cultures emphasise and reward individual achievement and expect individuals to focus on satisfying their own needs. The USA, the UK, Australia, New Zealand and the Netherlands are ranked among the most individualist countries. Highly collectivist cultures are found in Central and South America, Iran, India and Japan.

Collectivist cultures place great emphasis on group loyalty and the wider needs of the organisation or community to which an individual belongs. Individualism *v* collectivism is considered to be linked to religious values and beliefs. For example, in Europe collectivism is associated with Roman

Catholic countries whereas individualism appears to be more dominant amongst countries with Calvinist roots.

Masculinity v femininity

Masculine cultures emphasise and nurture values such as achievement, competitiveness, and assertion. Hofstede identified Japan as the most masculine culture. Australia, the UK, the USA, Germany, Italy and Switzerland are also considered strongly masculine cultures.

On the other hand, feminine cultures value co-operation rather than competition and are supportive and nurturing in their attitudes towards their members. The Scandinavian cultures of Sweden, Norway and Denmark are examples of very feminine cultures, and to a lesser extent those of Portugal and Spain.

More recently, Fons Trompenaars (1993) has identified seven fundamental dimensions of relationships between cultures and peoples. These are:

❑ *Universalism* v *particularism* – this refers to the extent to which rules (universalism) or relationships (particularism) dominate behaviour and influence the way in which members respond to moral dilemmas. In simple terms, this means that some cultures are more inclined to make exceptions to the rules than others. Universalist or rule-based behaviour is associated with cultures such as those of Canada, the USA, Switzerland and Germany, which consider that there should be universal standards which cultural members should live by. Particularist-oriented cultures are more characteristic of small, largely rural communities, eg Venezuela.

❑ *Individualism* v *collectivism* – this very much mirrors Hofstede's dimension.

❑ *Neutral* or *emotional* – this refers to the extent to which members of culture think and act in objective and detached ways as opposed to expressing emotions. Japan and Germany are considered to be examples of neutral cultures, whereas Italy and France are emotional.

- *Specific* v *diffuse* – this is concerned with relationships and the extent to which we generalise our behaviour towards an individual regardless of the circumstances in which we encounter them. In specific cultures, experience of an individual in one setting is considered a separate and distinct relationship. In specific cultures, there is a clear separation between work and private life. The UK, the USA, Australia and most of northern Europe are regarded as specific cultures. In diffuse cultures there is more of a spillover – your boss is always the boss in whatever circumstances you encounter him or her outside work. China typifies a diffuse culture.

- *Achievement* v *ascription* – this reflects the way in which cultures accord status to their members. Achievement cultures award status on the basis of 'doing', whereas ascription cultures award status on the basis of 'being' – ie attributes such as age, gender, social connections, education, etc. The USA is a high achievement culture whereas ascription cultures are more characteristic of underdeveloped and developing countries.

- *Attitudes to time* – some cultures focus more on what is going to happen in future (eg the USA) than what has happened in the past (eg France). According to Trompenaars, cultures also differ in the way they conceptualise time. Some cultures (eg the USA, Sweden) perceive time as being sequential, so that one event follows another in a straight line. Other cultures think of time as synchronic, as moving in a circle with past, present and future all interrelated.

- *Attitudes to the environment* – this final dimension concerns the extent to which cultures seek to control nature as opposed to going along with it, and is linked with the concept of the locus of control (LOC) discussed in Chapter 5. Again, the USA is identified as a culture which acts to control the natural environment, whereas China (for instance) has a more fatalistic approach.

Implications for mergers and acquisitions

In many ways consideration of these dimensions explains in part the preferences expressed by the managers in the study discussed earlier in this chapter (Cartwright, Cooper and Jordan, 1998). Northern European countries and the USA tend to cluster in their orientation towards individualism and low power distance, so demonstrating important areas of culture compatibility between them. As Table 7 shows, there is a great deal of similarity between the UK and the US business cultures which cannot be explained by language alone.

It is also clear that if two national cultures differ considerably in respect of all or most of these fundamental dimensions, any merger or acquisition between the two is likely to be extremely problematic.

Differences in orientation have implications for cross-border negotiations and integration management. Differences in core cultural values and attitudes will determine the emphasis and importance placed on different issues relating to any proposed cross-border M&A. Fons Trompenaars (1993) in his book *Riding the Waves of Culture* discusses each of the seven dimensions in great detail and provides practical tips for doing business, in the broader sense, with different national cultures.

In the context of cross-border M&A negotiations, the following guidelines are likely to be useful:

❑ Cultures with high power distance (eg France) will be most concerned about the proposed structure of the 'new'

Table 7
THE UK AND US CULTURES COMPARED

	British culture	US culture
Power distance	Low	Low
Uncertainty avoidance	Low	Low
Individualism	High	High
Masculinity	High	High
Universalism	Moderate	High
Specific	High	High
Achievement	High	Very high
Future-oriented	Moderate	High
Internally controlled	High	High

organisation and the way in which power and authority will be distributed. Characteristically, negotiations will be defensive as senior management seek to protect their existing power base.

- Risk-averse cultures (eg those of Greece, Portugal and Japan) will be looking for reassurances that change will be introduced gradually and that their members will not personally be held responsible if things go wrong, and so 'lose face'.

- Negotiations with collectivist cultures (eg Japan) are likely to be experienced by individualist cultures as highly frustrating because of their slow consultative decision-making style. Dealings with such cultures requires patience. It has to be recognised that trust and the establishment of a lasting relationship is of central importance to collectivist cultures, whereas individualist cultures want quick decisions.

- Highly feminine cultures (eg Scandinavia) place a high priority on human resource issues and the implications that the merger or acquisition will have on the quality of work life of employees.

- Universalist cultures (eg the USA, Germany) will be very keen to discuss the legal contractual aspects of the deal and will want to focus on as much detail as possible, whereas particularist cultures will want to focus more on relationships.

- Neutral cultures will want negotiations to be highly structured and will expect to be provided with supporting documentation prior to any meeting. In contrast, affective or emotional cultures will value and relate better to an informal negotiation style.

- Diffuse cultures are also often experienced by specific cultures as frustrating because of their tendency towards circuitous discussion. Again, it is important to exercise patience when negotiating with such cultures, and at the same time be respectful of status.

- Respect for status is also of central importance when negotiating with ascription-oriented cultures.

- Cultures with attitudes to time that are past-oriented will be concerned to retain symbols of their history and tradition. It may be necessary to consider the extent to which some of the symbols could be retained.

❑ Cultures which reflect an external locus of control are generally perceived by internally controlled cultures as somewhat passive. Indeed, they will often avoid challenge and conflict. However, it is important that disagreements and conflicts are brought out into the open, or there will be no genuine commitment to any proposed changes.

The culture of Italy is characterised by high power distance, strong uncertainty avoidance, high individualism and masculinity, and so differs from the UK's on two important dimensions: power and risk. As the following case-study illustrates, the sensitivity to these cultural differences became a key step in the formation of Marconi Communications.

Case-study

FORGING CULTURES: THE FORMATION OF MARCONI COMMUNICATIONS

GEC is undergoing a major restructuring following the Weinstock era, transforming itself into a focused high-technology, high-growth communications and IT company. To create the headroom and flexibility to realise this strategy, decisive moves have been made to reduce the dependence on joint ventures. One example of this was the flotation of Alsthom. Another, more importantly, was GEC's acquisition of Siemens' 40 per cent holding in GPT (GEC's largest telecoms company), which lay at the heart of the new strategy. Also, there has been a major move out of some traditional market sectors following the merging of GEC defence business with British Aerospace.

Having laid these foundations, the major thrust is to aggressively expand the telecoms business through growth, acquisitions and mergers. The first task was to integrate the two GEC telecoms businesses: GPT, which was predominantly UK-based, and Marconi SpA, which was predominantly Italian-based. Up to the acquisition of the Siemens' 40 per cent holding in GPT, these two organisations were competitors developing and selling similar product ranges in similar markets. However, GPT was the larger of the two and held dominance in the fast-expanding UK market.

The synergies of these two organisations were clear from the start: the real benefits of rationalising the product ranges and customer base; the strength of the combined technologies and engineering resource; the advantages of the combined routes to market, both direct and indirect; and the benefits of consolidation in the supply chain. The real task was to integrate the two organisations into a single trading entity, leveraging efficiencies, consolidating the market position and focusing on common goals.

With the first line management team consisting of a majority of UK nationals, and with the UK organisation being larger, there was an understandable perception from the Italians that this was a UK takeover. There was a very conscious effort therefore to involve and include Italians in all the senior management teams. The current chairman is Italian and the managing director is British. Positively, many teams – account management, engineering, finance, the supply chain, etc – now consist of both UK and Italian nationals.

Every effort has been made by the management team to engage the 'new organisation' with communication events and conferences. The senior management conference was deliberately held in Milan this year. Language and cultural training has been actively promoted, with healthy levels of participation achieved.

An integration project was formed which had a mix of both UK and Italian nationals. The objective was to define and implement a common set of business processes and values, which would capture best practice from both organisations and externally.

All these initiatives and more have helped considerably in bringing both parts of the organisation together in a relatively short period of time, while meeting the demands of the day-to-day business and achieving aggressive growth targets.

This is all positive stuff, but integration is hard – it can't be viewed as a programme – it has to be a 'continuum'. There have been barriers to progress – dismay when plans are agreed and nothing happens, recriminations when things go wrong – in fact, the normal stresses all organisations experience. In some cases, a distinct lack of harmony when individual approaches are taken rather than a common approach.

In retrospect, one of the biggest barriers was the lack of understanding of the national cultures. In fact, insensitivity to cultural differences, and not modifying approaches accordingly, has been an impediment. Fundamentally, all cultures protect themselves, and this principle has to be taken into account when undertaking any integration activities.

What we have uncovered is the strong UK or Anglo-Saxon view of 'What is right and works for us is right for everybody else.' An imposition of this nature is not an effective strategy, especially when dealing with Mediterranean cultures. This single-mindedness is a strength, but when applied insensitively it earns a reputation for arrogance.

To exemplify this, the interaction of debate and discussion to reach an outcome involving Italian colleagues is interesting. Their perception of their British counterparts is that views are invited, politely discussed and possibly agreed which are then subsequently ignored. They call this 'sophisticated arrogance'. It was not intentional, but it is insensitive. The Italian approach is a noisy and possibly lengthy debate, which ultimately produces an outcome that is agreed and supported by all the participants.

The UK business culture has process structures and rules which, you can argue, is necessary to manage the complexity of business today. This has the advantage of control and visibility, with a degree of openness from UK managers on issues and problems. This influence has, as one might expect, been promoted within the Italian part of the organisation – and met with some resistance. They are not averse to 'process' but see the UK as overdoing it to the brink of bureaucracy and inflexibility.

The Italians' great strength is teamwork, informality, innovation and flexibility, the ability to realise their goals without the formality of process and controls. From a UK perspective, this can appear chaotic, with little control on outputs compounded with the Italian desire to please and give a good story which can disguise the real situation. You can imagine the frustrations this causes. However, there would be greater benefit from a little more structure and process in these situations.

The strong Italian family ethic has distinct advantages in a range of business activities and relationships. However, it is hierarchical, with great respect given to those with title and position, which makes it an intriguing exercise when decision-making and executing actions. The UK culture tends to be more democratic in this respect. Even so, there are still too many decisions that are escalated to the top and not dealt with at the operative level.

It is interesting in respect of the progress on integration that there are many UK nationals working in Italy and very few Italians based in the UK. It was explained that although there was a desire for the Italians to be more mobile, there is a strong loyalty to the existing group and a fear of future exclusion if a decision to move was made.

There are no right or wrong answers. There has to be an ongoing programme of organisational development which recognises the flaws and addresses them. Integration is a process of learning, application and communication while being sensitive to the cultural differences and working to put these to advantage.

The big lesson learnt is that Anglo-Saxon autocracy and imposition is ineffective. Integration is about addressing common issues together with excellent and regular communication by everyone.

Integration is working for Marconi Communications. It is rewarding to see the high degree of joint participation and growing mutual respect. However, this is the beginning of the journey, and there is still much to be done.

Every acquisition merger and integration is different, depending upon the objectives. I have given an insight into some of the obvious pitfalls to full integration.

Other acquisitions may be specifically focused on securing a route to market or buying a new technology. The strategy may well be to have only a high-level interface which supports the strengths of the local culture and knowledge.

With the ever-quickening pace of change, especially in telecoms, speed is of the essence in the acquisition process. Newly-joined businesses need to be aligned quickly so that business goals and efficiencies can start to be realised at the earliest opportunity. This has to be driven by a hard-hitting plan. Shareholders expect nothing less.

Cultures are difficult or impossible to change. You may modify behaviour, though – so sensitivity and understanding of culture is essential in order that the strengths of each can be played to advantage in the business.

Source: Jeremy Grammer, director of performance management, Marconi Communications

Summary

The provision of some form of cross-cultural training is vital to assist cross-border partners in understanding the way in which they 'see the world' and to recognise their different value systems. Acquiring or merging organisations need to be made aware of their own cultural paradigm as well as that of the partnering organisation. There are several useful texts (for example, Gesteland, 1999) which provide country-by-country information and advice on marketing, negotiating and managing cross-cultures. Some, such as Mead (1990), specifically focus on cross-cultural management communication.

Mead places particular importance on encouraging organisations to provide language training. Too often, he argues, English-speaking companies adopt the attitude 'My language is the international language of business. Let them learn my language rather than me learn theirs.' Language training is costly and time-consuming. However, Mead cites the example of the General Foam Division of Tenneco Inc, USA, where such training made a measurable contribution to organisational performance. Some 75 per cent of the workforce of General Foam were Spanish-speaking and the labour turnover rate was between 30 and 40 per cent, when English language training was introduced. The classes had an immediate and positive effect in reducing accident rates, improving production and reducing the number of union grievances and employee complaints.

References

ATTENDORF D. M. (1986) 'When cultures clash: a case study of the Texaco takeover of Getty Oil and the impact of acculturation on the acquired firm'. Unpublished dissertation, University of Southern California. August.

CARTWRIGHT S. *and* COOPER C. L. (1996) *Managing Mergers, Acquisitions and Strategic Alliances: Integrating people and cultures*. Oxford, Butterworth-Heinemann.

CARTWRIGHT S., COOPER C. L. *and* JORDAN J. (1998) 'Managerial preferences in international merger and acquisition partners', in D. Hussey (ed.), *The Strategic Decision Challenge*, Chichester, John Wiley & Sons.

GESTELAND R. R. (1999) *Cross-Cultural Business Behaviour.* Copenhagen, Handelshøjskolens Forlag (Copenhagen Business College Press).

HOFSTEDE G. (1980) *Culture Consequences.* Beverly Hills, CA, Sage Publications.

INTERNATIONAL SURVEY RESEARCH (1999) *How is the Coming Together Going! Managing motivation in the multi-national merger.* ISR.

MEAD R. (1990) *Cross-Cultural Management Communication.* Chichester, John Wiley & Sons.

OLIE R. (1990) 'Culture and integration problems in international mergers and acquisitions'. *European Management Journal.* 8(2). pp206–315.

TROMPENAARS F. (1993) *Riding the Waves of Culture: Understanding cultural diversity in business.* London, Nicholas Brealey.

9 A FINAL WORD: MONITORING THE ONGOING PROCESS OF INTEGRATION

One of the major problems in assessing merger and acquisition gains is that it is difficult to decide upon the appropriate time period over which to conduct that assessment. However, it is reasonable to take the view that it will be at least two years before the acquired or merged organisation will have regained some form of stability so that organisational members will no longer attribute what is happening in the company to be 'merger-related'.

The early stages of the integration period will be busy and exhausting times for the HRM team. Once new policies and systems have been put in place, training needs have been addressed and employment problems have been resolved, it is easy to sit back and think that the merger is now 'done and dusted'.

However, such complacency should be avoided and it is important to regularly monitor and revisit employee issues and concerns. Systems need to be set up to deal with post-merger grievances which may surface over time. Initiatives to monitor employee attitudes, staff turnover, stress levels and satisfaction with communication processes need to remain in place to enable HRM to identify functional areas or employee groups where problems may be developing. As well as monitoring internal cohesion, it is important to remain in close touch with external suppliers, customers and clients to ensure that performance standards and service levels are being met and that the merged organisation is acting in a consistent way towards its external environment. As Paul Hodder, HR director of Aon Risk Services stated in Chapter 7, 'Nobody gets everything right; the important point is whether an organisation consolidates and shares what it has learnt.' It is the role of HRM to get managers together and conduct a post-merger review. This is the most effective way to bring that learning together and ensure that it is passed on to future M&A management teams. In a recent article on the M&A success, David Hussey (1998), writing in the *Journal of Professional HRM*, observes:

> I am still puzzled why so many managers have failed to learn from the experiences of others. After all, there is little in the current [1998 survey] research that was not discovered 20 to 30 years ago. Will we ever learn?

Making a good organisational marriage should not be a matter of chance or luck; the stakes are much too high. Successful M&As, like successful and enduring partnerships of any kind, are achieved through hard work, patience, tolerant attitudes, understanding and good communication. As, hopefully, this book has demonstrated, good management rather than any matchmaker's spell or alchemist's dust is the key to success.

Reference

HUSSEY D. (1998) 'Is acquisition and merger a successful strategy?' *Journal of Professional HRM*. 13. October. pp3–10.

Index